Bradford K. Peirce

The Word of God Opened

Its inspiration, canon, and interpretation considered and illustrated

Bradford K. Peirce

The Word of God Opened

Its inspiration, canon, and interpretation considered and illustrated

ISBN/EAN: 9783337184025

Printed in Europe, USA, Canada, Australia, Japan

Cover: Foto ©Lupo / pixelio.de

More available books at **www.hansebooks.com**

WORD OF GOD OPENED.

ITS

INSPIRATION, CANON, AND INTERPRETATION
CONSIDERED AND ILLUSTRATED.

By BRADFORD K. PEIRCE, D.D.

"Open thou mine eyes,
That I may behold wondrous things out of thy law."

"Qui hæret in litera hæret in cortice."

NEW YORK: HUNT & EATON.
CINCINNATI: CRANSTON & STOWE.
1889.

PREFACE.

THE writer of this volume has sought to place in the hands of young students, and interpreters of the Bible who are not familiar with the original tongues in which the Holy Scriptures were written, or favored with an easy access to the treasures of sacred criticism which are constantly accumulating, such evidences of the authenticity, genuineness, and general purity of the English version of the Old and New Testaments, arising out of its history and the searching examinations to which it has been submitted, that they may open it with confidence to discover in its revelations the mind of the Spirit. He has sought, also, to set forth and illustrate the nature of its inspiration, the most obvious preliminary studies and preparations for a safe interpretation of its contents, and the most important rules for the guidance of the interpreter in his work. The writer has not proposed fully to enter upon the argument on which rests the confirmed judgment of evangelical Christians upon these topics, but to indicate and illustrate the various steps in it, so that the Bible student will be enabled to have a clear comprehension of its nature and force; and, at his leisure, to turn to the abundant authorities crowding our Christian literature for an exhaustive examination of these questions.

The author has sought constantly to keep in view the great class of teachers just now awakened to earnest inquiry as to the means of meeting the serious requisitions made upon them as interpreters of the word of God to the children of our land, and to prepare his volume in such a way as best to aid them in their work.

He has availed himself of such sources of information as he could secure in the various branches of biblical criticism involved in his work, and has rendered credit to them in the body of the volume. Special aid has been derived from the Hermeneutical Manual of Dr. Fairbairn, and from the admirable works of the same author upon Prophecy and Typology. Valuable suggestions have been gleaned from Alford's Prolegomena to his Greek Testament, and his interesting work under the title of How to Study the New Testament; from Nast's General Introduction to the Gospels; from Prof. Murphy's Introduction to his Commentary upon Genesis; from Schaff's History of the Christian Church; from Westcott's invaluable Introduction to the Study of the New Testament, and his History of the Canon; from Horne; from Davidson; from Cowper's Apocryphal Gospels; and from the Boyle Lectures for 1866 on Christ and Christendom by Plumptre. Rev. David Dobie has written a strong, original, and sprightly work upon interpretation, entitled "A Key to the Bible;" but its rules of interpretation are unnecessarily multiplied, and nearly all of them singularly tend to elaborate from Scripture one modern system of theology. Its illustrations have been of great service to the writer. Prof. M'Lelland's work upon the Canon and Interpretation of the Scriptures has been laid under contribution for the same purpose; as also Gaussen upon the Canon. A scientific and comprehensive work upon the Hermeneutics of the New Testament by a Dutch clergyman, Dr. Doedes, has been consulted with profit; and a late English work by J. Radford Thomson upon Symbols. We owe, and are happy to express, special obligation to Dr. Goulburn for his rich little treatise upon the Devotional Study of the Bible. Much assistance has been rendered by the Hand-Book of the Bible of Angus. The works of Stanley and Milman, and the various Biblical Encyclopædias and Dictionaries, have been examined, as their valuable contents have offered aid in the work.

We trust that our labor, which has from first to last been a labor of love, will not be in vain, but that our little volume may become a guide to many young explorers among the hidden mines and treasures of Holy Scripture.

B. K. PEIRCE.

RIVERSIDE PARSONAGE,
   RANDALL'S ISLAND, *March*, 1868.

CONTENTS.

CHAPTER I.
THE BIBLE.

God revealed by Inspired Men, and by an Inspired Book—In Harmony with the Creation of the World—Light first, and then the Sun—Written Scriptures commence with Moses—Like the Sun and Stars, they become permanent Sources of Revelation—The same Truth is illustrated in the New Testament Scriptures—Inspired Men first, and then Inspired Books—The Holy Spirit closed the Canon—Error of Edward Irving—Folly of Spiritualists—The "Inner Light" never superior to the Bible—Bible only Rule of Faith—Necessity for an infallible Rule....................Page 13

CHAPTER II.
INSPIRATION.

God the Author, Men the Writers, of the Bible—Oldest Volume in the World—Various Authors and Styles—Teachings of all Harmonize—Writers were not acquainted with the Sciences—Used a simple, figurative, and poetic Form of Expression adapted to all Ages—They claim to be Inspired—Established by their Veracity—Human Authorship impossible from nature of Revelations—Words not necessarily Inspired—Dr. Schaff's view—Verbal Inspiration would require a constant Miracle—Varied forms of Inspiration illustrated—Alford's view of Inspiration—The Scripture view of Inspiration by Prof. Murphy.................................... 19

CHAPTER III.
THE CANON: ITS GENUINENESS.

Is our English Bible the word of God Revealed?—Original Language of the Old Testament—Apocrypha—Care taken by the Jews to preserve the Purity of the Scriptures—Philo and Josephus—

Samaritan Pentateuch — Spread of the Greek Language over Bible Lands — Jews in Egypt — The Septuagint — This Version was used by Christ — The Syriac or Peshito Version — Italic — Origen and his Version — Jerome — The Vulgate — Its gradual introduction into the Roman Church — The first book printed — Declared infallible by the Council of Trent — Different Editions of it — Various Versions of the Scriptures — New Testament Canon — First Oral Communications from Inspired Men — Many Records were made, all but the Four Gospels have disappeared — Matthew — Characteristics of his Gospel — Mark — His Epistle written under the Sanction of Peter — Evidently the Gospel of an Eye-witness — Luke writes under the direction of Paul — Resident of Antioch — Sources of his Gospel — Whence account of the Nativity derived — John wrote last — Call for his Gospel in the false views of Christ prevalent in the Churches — A marvelous Book, when it is recollected its Human Author was a Fisherman — Paul's Epistles — Peter affirms them to be Inspired — Testimony of Papias to the Gospels - Irenæus — Tertullian — Justin Martyr — The Syriac Version — Origen — Pamphilius — Eusebius — Constantine the Great orders fifty Copies of the Septuagint to be prepared by Eusebius and circulated among the Churches — Some Books of the New Testament for a while held in suspense — Apocryphal Books of the New Testament — Use of them — Character of them — First English Version by Wiclif — First printed Version by Tyndale — Sufferings and Martyrdom of Tyndale — Fate of his Work — Edition by John Rogers — Coverdale's Bible — Effect of circulating Bible in England — Froude's opinion of Tyndale's Version — Douay Version — Martin Luther — Influence upon Biblical Criticism — German Version — The Authorized English Version — Effect of Revival of Letters upon Biblical Criticism — Fears at first entertained — Olshausen — Bengel — Fears entirely removed — Nature of Variations — Prof. Norton upon Purity of Text.................Page 31

CHAPTER IV.

INTERPRETATION: GENERAL OBSERVATIONS.

Hermeneutics — Office of Biblical Interpretation — Peculiarities of the Bible rendering its interpretation difficult — Why was it given in this Form? — Analogy with Human Life — Dr. Schaff on the Character of the Bible — Locke on things difficult to be understood — Wonderful things in Nature hidden from our sight — Difficulty and Mystery add to the interest of Scripture — Exertion required to obtain the Treasures of Nature — Hidden Truths of Scripture — Bible presents Facts and Principles, but does not make

Moral Applications — Distinction between Attention and Thought — Failure in Sunday-schools — Devotional Thought — The whole Bible should be studied — Christ in the whole Bible — Revelation Progressive — Dr. Chalmers upon Progress in Moral Consciousness — Progress in the New Testament — Olshausen upon Unity and Progress in Scripture — Locke on reading a Book of Scripture through at a sitting — Sacred Writers sometimes state their object — Beauty and Power of Scripture lost when taken from its connections — Each Gospel has a Character of its own — Scripture is not a Revelation of Science — Dr. Stowe on the unscientific Character of the Bible — Folly of interpreting Genesis as a Treatise upon Geology — Common-sense an interpreter of the Bible — True Science cannot harm the Bible — The Bible is not a "Body of Divinity" — Different Truths are taught in different places — Goulburn's illustration of this from Nature — Error of Rationalists and Universalists — Interpreter not Responsible for what God says — Dr. Doedes upon this irresponsibility — Error of early Interpreters — Fanciful Interpretations — Reformation changed this — Illustrations of Ancient Interpretation — Historico-Grammatical Interpretation.....................Page 68

CHAPTER V.

PRELIMINARY STUDIES.

Study of Ancient Languages — Importance of a Knowledge of Biblical Geography — Renan — Hibbard and Vincent — Effect of Pilgrimages to the Holy Land — Dean Stanley's Account of the Vicinity of Hebron — Works upon Bible Geography — Value in the interpretation of Prophecy — The Cities of Bashan — Rev. J. L. Porter in Bashan — Present appearance of the Country — John L. Stephens in Petra — Fulfillment of Prophecy — Most interesting reading for the Young — Customs and Manners of the East — Sir S. W. Baker — Song of Solomon — Parables — Sitting at Table — Breaking of Bread — Symbols — The Ceremonial Law — Symbols carried to Extremes — Symbolical Numbers — Natural Symbols — Animal Symbols — Jerusalem and Babylon — Earthly Royalty — The Vintage and Harvest — Harps, Keys, and Book — The Bride — Battle of Armageddon — Symbolical Acts — Marriage of Prophet to Prophetess — Symbols of Hosea and Ezekiel — Symbols should be interpreted with care — Must be in sympathy with the Sacred Writers — Hagenbach on inward interest — Dr. Paulus — Why so little interest in the Bible? — Man needs the Holy Spirit — Illustrated by Sun Dial — The Spirit acts *through* the Human Mind.. 100

CHAPTER VI.
RULES OF INTERPRETATION.

Rule I — The Obvious Meaning of the Words the True One — Bengel on holding to the Text — Melanchthon on the Sense of Scripture — Luther's view — Writers, humble, open, and sincere. Remark 1. When an Impossibility seems to be asserted, it is not to be taken literally — Illustrations of this — The Body and Blood of Christ in the Sacrament — How to know a figurative Expression — "Buried with him in Baptism." Remark 2. The Meaning must not contradict our Moral Sense — Figurative Precepts — "Many *made* Sinners" — What the Apostle teaches in reference to this — "The Wicked *made* for the Day of Evil" — Nothing Contradictory to our Moral Convictions. Remark 3. Anything Contradictory to Universal Experience must be Modified. Remark 4. Poetry and Prophecy must not be interpreted literally. Rule II. The Meaning of the Words must be taken in accordance with the Usages of Speech at the time they were Uttered — Changes in our own Language — Bearing our own and others' Burdens — The Power of Christ resting upon one — Hebraisms — Things said to be done when attempted — One who Occasions an Act said to do it — Difficult things said to be Impossible — Passages referring Human Acts to God — Names of Parents used for Descendants — Relatives called Brothers. Rule III. By the Use of Parallel Passages the Bible should be made its own Expositor — Importance of Reference Bible — Bishop Horsley on comparison of Scripture with Scripture — True meaning of Doctrines thus Discovered — Error of Jews — Must compare like Terms — Import of the term Baptize — How to use Parallel Passages — Scripture Terms often have Different Significations — Gospel Writers Supplement each other — The "Strait Gate" — Context must be carefully examined — The Messianic Psalms — No Doctrine should be Built up on Separate Clauses of Scripture — The Prodigal Son and the Address to Nicodemus — Dying in Adam, Living in Christ — The strongest meaning not always the correct one — Perverted Texts — Scripture distinctly presents both Human and Divine Nature of Christ. Rule IV. All Scripture must be interpreted in Harmony with the Analogy of Faith — All apparent discrepancies must be harmonized in accordance with this Rule — False foundation of Papal Purgatory — Passages referring to God after the manner of Men — Why God is thus spoken of — "Upon this rock I will build my Church" — "Covering a multitude of Sins" — Scripture Difficulties no occasion for Discouragement — Abundant answers to all Difficulties — Never give an unsatisfactory Answer — Dean Alford upon Discrepancies of the New Testament — Henry Rogers upon the same. Rule V. The Spiritual Meaning is to be earnestly Sought After — Bible given for a Special Purpose — God teaches some Lesson in every portion — Error of Ernesti and Grotius — Westcott on Spiritual Interpretation — The view of Horne .... Page 124

CHAPTER VII.
INTERPRETATION OF PARABLE, POETRY, AND PROPHECY.

Principal Parables delivered in the last year of our Lord's Life — Distinguishing marks of his Parables — Reasons for using them — View of Tholuck — Aid in remembering Discourses — Powerfully impressed the Truth — Used to vail Truth, because it had been Neglected — Analogous to all Christ's Work — Mr. Gladstone's view of the Parables — Christ supreme in them — First Rule: Must fully Understand the Parable in all its parts — Second Rule: Discover from the context the Exact Truth to be Illustrated — Lisco on the Kernel of the Parable — Lesson of the Parables in the fifteenth of Luke — Parable of the Rich Fool — Of the Householder and his Laborers — Third Rule: The separate parts of the Parable should not be considered out of their relation to the Story — Apt to overdo in Interpretation — Illustrated from Trench — Much of the Bible Poetic — Easily remembered — Sir Patrick Hume — Psalms sung in all Times --They are to be interpreted according to the Laws of Rhetoric — A Doctrinal Statement not to be built up on Figurative Language — Illustrations from Psalms — Literal rendering of some shown to be Absurd — To be interpreted in sympathy with the feelings of the Psalmist — Poetry of the Imagination and of the Affections — The Times and Circumstances of their Composition throw light upon their Interpretation — Dr. Townsend's Arrangement — Illustration from Stanley's History of the Jewish Church — Parallelism of the Psalms, Synonomous, Antithetic, Synthetic — The Vindictive Psalms not expressions of Personal Wrath — The Songs of the Persecuted of all Ages — Dr. Park's Illustration from the late War — Proverbs and Ecclesiastes are Divine Repositories of Moral Maxims — Solomon's Song — Isaac Taylor's View — Prophecy abounds in the Bible — Illustrative Events said to be the Fulfillment — Rachel weeping — Calling out of Egypt — History fulfilled Prophecy — Prophet no idea of Time — Jesus did not appeal to Figures — Prophecies of New Testament — Prophecy not History — Hour of Christ's second coming not Revealed — Irving's Error — Dr

Cumming — What the Bible teaches in reference to the End of the World — Prophecy a profitable Study — A grand Epic — Dr. Schaff's View...Page 167

CHAPTER VIII.
THE BIBLE IN THE WORLD'S LITERATURE.

Never before so widely Circulated — Bitter attack made upon it — Foes under the garb of Friends — Object of Attack, Christ and God's Word — We have no occasion for anxiety — the Bible has gained from these attacks — Its literature prodigious — Compared with Shakspeare — The latter owes much to the Bible — Gray's Elegy compared with the Twenty-third Psalm — Henry Stephanus on Psalms — John von Mueller — Alexander von Humboldt — Goethe — Its hold upon the most powerful Minds — Rousseau — Coleridge — Carlyle — Bishop Butler — Wilberforce — Webster — Sir Francis Bacon — Milton — Newton — Lord Erskine — Guizot — Talleyrand — No other Book can take the place of the Bible — Such a Book cannot die — Walter Scott's Bible Motto..................... 207

THE
WORD OF GOD OPENED.

CHAPTER I.

THE BIBLE.

GOD revealed himself and his will, at first, to man by inspired men; "holy men of God spake as they were moved by the Holy Ghost."[1] Afterward he caused these revelations to be gathered into an inspired book: "All Scripture is given by inspiration of God."[2] This course is in wonderful harmony with the divine economy in the creation of the world. Light was formed upon the first day; "in the beginning . . . God said, Let there be light."[3] This light was diffused through chaotic nature, emanating from no local or material fountains: "and God saw the light that it was good." It was not until the fourth day that these floods of light were collected into suns and fixed stars, and became ever after the divinely-appointed sources of illumination. "And God said, Let there be lights in the firmament of the heaven to divide the day from the night . . . and the evening and the morning were the fourth day."[4]

God revealed by inspired men and by an inspired book.

In harmony with the creation of the world.

[1] 2 Peter i, 21.   [2] 2 Tim. iii, 16.   [3] Gen. i, 1, 3.   [4] Gen. i, 14–19.

For twenty-five hundred years, until the time of Moses, religious light was diffused and faint, kindled by direct communications of God to favored individuals; but in his day God began to cause permanent lights, in the form of written Scriptures, to take their lasting places in the moral firmament, to shed their divine beams upon human hearts, and to "divide the light from the darkness." Like the sun and stars, they have held their places unmoved, constantly shedding forth their light over the origin, decay, and destruction of human governments and the proudest works of man: "Heaven and earth shall pass away," but these "words" of divine revelation "shall not pass away."[5]

Written Scriptures commence with Moses.

These lights are permanent.

After the same analogy, the Scriptures of the New Testament were given. God spake first by inspired men and by direct communications. The promise of the former covenant was, "In the last days (the times of the Messiah) I will pour out of my Spirit upon all flesh, and your sons and your daughters shall prophesy, and your young men shall see visions, and your old men dream dreams; and on my servants and on my handmaidens I will pour out in those days of my Spirit, and they shall prophesy;"[6] that is, they shall declare the revelations of God—the Gospel—under the immediate inspiration of the Holy Ghost.[7] This promise was literally fulfilled. At first, upon all that believed,

The same truth illustrated in the New Testament Scriptures.

Prophecy of the Messiah's times.

---

[5] Matt. xxiv, 35.   [6] Acts ii, 17, 18.

[7] See Introduction to Study of Holy Scriptures, by Dr. Goulburn, Article B, in Appendix.

miraculous powers of speaking or specific revelations of truth from the Holy Ghost were bestowed indiscriminately, as upon the company of believers at Pentecost, and afterward [8] upon the Roman centurion and the company collected in his house; [9] upon the disciples scattered by persecution from Jerusalem,[10] and apparently wherever the apostles first introduced the preaching of the Gospel. The virgin daughters of Philip the evangelist were endowed with this divine gift,[11] and Priscilla united with her husband Aquila, then in Athens, driven by persecution from Rome, in expounding "the way of God more perfectly" to the eloquent Apollos, a Jew of Alexandria, himself mighty in the Hebrew Scriptures.[12] *This prophecy fulfilled.*

But by divine inspiration this diffused light was collected into permanent orbs. God no longer made personal revelations of truth to individuals' minds, but directed his chosen instruments to embody, under the guidance of the Holy Spirit,[13] such an expression of his truth as he desired to have made to the world. He closed himself the work of inspired revelation with the solemn words, "If any man shall add unto these things, God shall add unto him the plagues that are written in this book; and if any man shall take away from the words of the book of this prophecy, God shall take away his part out of the book of life, and out of the holy city, and from the things which are written in this book." [14] *Collected in a permanent form.* *The Holy Spirit closed the canon.*

In overlooking this truth, so in harmony with the divine

[8] Acts ii, 4; iv, 31.   [9] Acts x, 44-46.   [10] Acts xi, 19, 21.   [11] Acts xxi, 9.
[12] Acts xviii, 24-26.   [13] John xiv, 26.   [14] Rev. xxii, 18, 19.

processes in the natural world, taught in the Scriptures themselves, and confirmed by the history of the Church, the eloquent and devoted Edward Irving, and his sincere but misguided followers, in England, turned the worship of the sanctuary into a babel of unmeaning sounds, and blasphemously attributed to that Spirit who brought order out of chaos, the awful and insane jargon of tongues which drove every rational worshiper from the house of God.

<small>*Error of Edward Irving.*</small>

The same condemnation must be declared against those in modern times, of a coarser mold, less scholarly, and far less pious, (however sincere some may be, and however bewildered by strange physical phenomena, the laws of which are not clearly understood,) who suppose that they have, or pretend that they have, communication with the world of spirits. They are self-deceived, or their minds are perverted by the devil. God does not reveal his truth in this way, "for God is not the author of confusion, but of peace." [15]

<small>*Folly of "Spiritualists"*</small>

This view of divine truth is opposed to the doctrine of those who hold that any "inner light" with which they are favored can take the place of the Bible as a rule of life. The Holy Spirit cannot deny himself; and having *spoken* harmoniously through a long line of chosen men, and having himself closed the canon of inspiration, he will not contradict this revelation in the hearts of believers. "Thy word," said the Psalmist more than twenty-eight hundred years ago, before even the Old Testa-

<small>*The "inner light" not above the Bible.*</small>

---

[15] 1 Corinthians xiv, 38.

THE WORD OF GOD OPENED.

ment Scriptures had been closed, "is a lamp unto my feet, and a light unto my path."[16]

The Bible, not as explained by commentators, or held by any particular branch of the Church, or illustrated by tradition, or confirmed by human reason, but as given by God through the holy men that wrote its pages, and truthfully interpreted from their lips, is our infallible rule of faith and practice. *The Bible the alone rule of faith and practice.*

Of the necessity of this great superhuman orb of light, Dr. Goulburn remarks that it arises from man's "utter mental darkness as to his destiny, as to his duties, and as to his dangers; above all, as to the method in which he must be saved. A revelation upon these points must be made to him by God if his feet are to be set upon the way that leadeth unto life. That need is represented by imagining men in a state of natural darkness, unrelieved save by a few twinkling stars. Let the faint and feeble ray of these stars represent all the aid which man can get from what is proudly called the moral sense; that is, his innate notions of right and wrong. Can you see objects by starlight in their true colors? Can you avoid pitfalls and marshes and stumbling-blocks by starlight? Can you do any work effectually by starlight? or is it not rather true that we must work while we have sunlight; and that when the night cometh no man can work? In a similar manner we see not good and evil in their true colors; we are ignorant of the tremendous danger of sinful courses, ignorant of the traps which Satan sets in our way, ignorant of how to *Necessity for this infallible rule.*

[16] Psalm cxix, 105.

serve God properly, and as he would be served, without instruction from above on these and similar points. We must have light, and this light is called revelation, the revelation under which we live (or Christian revelation) being the clearest and best ever yet vouchsafed to the world." [17]

[17] Devotional Study of the Scriptures, p. 184.

CHAPTER II.

INSPIRATION.

THE Bible claims God as its author, but all its pages were written by human hands, and bear the significant marks of the different writers. Its various books were written at different periods, often with long lapses of time between them. Its first records, the five books attributed to Moses, and called from their number in Greek the Pentateuch, were written more than thirty-three hundred years ago—fifteen hundred years before Christ; its last book is supposed to have been completed in the year of our Lord one hundred. It was, therefore, during the long period of sixteen hundred years that the work of revelation was going on.   *God the author, men the writers of the Bible.*

The Bible contains the oldest writings in the world. The most ancient human histories now in existence, those of Herodotus and Thucydides, were written a thousand years after the times of Moses. It is composed of sixty-six different books, and was written by, at least, forty different authors. It is generally written in the language of common life, but always in a style of commanding simplicity and dignity. Its human authors filled almost every position in life from the humblest to the most exalted. The peculiarities of the writers, their cultivation or lack of it, the times in which   *Bible the oldest volume in the world.*   *Various authors and different styles.*

they lived, the dialect they used, the station they filled, their gradual advance in divine illumination, are all disclosed in the various books forming the completed revelation of the will of God to man. Some of the books are historical, some of them summaries of religious rites, some genealogical, others dramatical and poetical, and others still in highly-wrought and sublime figures embody prophecies stretching through all ages. The wonderful truth in reference to them all is, that, when thus brought together from so many sources, from so many ages, in so many styles, and composed separately without reference to their final collection in one volume, there should be found throughout them all an absolute harmony in their revelations of the character and purposes of God, of the nature and necessities of man, and of the one great, divine plan of human redemption. Each portion seems to be naturally related to the others, and has an important office to perform in completing the perfect and harmonious scheme.

Character of the different books.

All harmonious in their teachings.

In every respect, excepting their remarkable knowledge of divine truths, the Scripture writers were like their neighbors. They had no special knowledge above their fellows as to general science and history. They did not pronounce their revelations in a scientific form. If this had not been the case, Dean Milman[1] remarks, how utterly unintelligible would their words have been to their fellow-men! Conceive of a prophet, or psalmist, or an apostle, endowed with premature knowledge, and talking of the various geological periods in the history of the earth, or

Writers of the Bible not acquainted with science.

[1] History of Jews. Preface to revised edition. Vol. 1, pp. 17-19.

of the planetary system according to the Newtonian laws, instead of simply declaring "in the beginning God created the heavens and the earth," and speaking of the "sun going forth as a bridegroom to run his course!" They disclosed the mighty truths of God in the common and ordinarily picturesque and poetic language of the days in which they lived. This form, requiring now careful study and reflection to apprehend its exact meaning, was *Clothed in figurative and poetic language.* inseparable from their daily life, and the only common medium for the conveyance of revelation to all ages. In no other form, humanly speaking, would they have struck so deep into the mind and heart of man, or clung to it with such inseverable tenacity. It is as speaking frequently in the noblest poetry, and constantly addressing the imaginative as well as the reasoning faculty of man, that these Scriptures have survived through ages, and have been and are still imperishable when considered only as the work of human minds. As the teachers were men of their age in all but religious advancement, so their books were the books of their age. They were the oracles of God in their divine instructions, while the language in which they were spoken was human, and uttered in a style to be understood by the half-enlightened people for whose benefit they were first declared; and, what is still more sig- *Revelation is thus adapted to all ages.* nificant of their divine origin, revealing clearly the same truths in an impressive manner to races of different customs and tongues far advanced in civilization, and familiar with the amazing disclosures of modern science.

Although speaking in their own natural style, and giving

utterance often to their own personal emotions, or simply recording events passing under their eyes, the writers claim for themselves and affirm of each other that their records contain the words of God, and are uttered under his inspiration.

The writers claim to be inspired.

In no other way can their unity and harmony be accounted for. "If the Scriptures are not the word of God," says Professor Murphy in the introduction to his comments upon Genesis, "then the writers of these Scriptures, who directly and indirectly affirm their divine origin are false witnesses; and if they have proved unworthy of credit in this fundamental point, they can be of no authority on other equally important matters. But neither before examination, nor after an examination of eighteen centuries, have we the slightest reason for doubting the veracity of these men, and their unanimous evidence is in favor of the divine authorship of the Bible. All that we have learned of the contents of these books accords with their claim to be the word of God. The constant harmony of their statements when fairly interpreted with one another, with general history, and with physical and metaphysical truth, affords an incontestable proof of their divine origin. The statements of other early writers have invariably come into conflict with historical or scientific truth. But still further, these books communicate to us matters concerning God, the origin and the future destiny of man, which are of vital importance in themselves, and yet are absolutely beyond the reach of human intuition, observation, or deduction. It is

Claim to inspiration established by veracity of the writers.

Harmony of revelation with natural laws.

Human authorship impossible.

impossible, therefore, for mere human beings, apart from divine instruction and authority, to attest these things to us at all. Hence these books, if they were not traceable ultimately to a divine author, would absolutely fail us in the very points that are essential to be known, namely, the origin of our being, the relation in which we stand to God, and the way to eternal happiness, on which neither science nor history afford us any light. But they yield a clear, definite, and consistent light and help, meeting the very askings and longings of our souls on these momentous topics. *They meet the great wants of our nature.* The wonderful way in which they convince the reason, probe the conscience, and apply a healing balm to the wounded spirit, is in itself an independent attestation to their divine origin." [2]

The Bible is not a specimen of the style of the Holy Spirit as a writer; but the different authors expressed in their own language and by their own illustrations the ideas poured into their minds from on high. *The Bible not a specimen of God's style.* The revelation is perfect and plenary, for it is divine; but the medium is imperfect and exposes its human limitations and weaknesses, and so much the more confirms the divine origin of the truths that are taught. If each word, as some teach, was inspired, then the writers were *Words not necessarily inspired.* simply amanuenses, and every book of Scripture, like the Ten Commandments, is a specimen of divine and not human composition. The Son of man was no less a perfect man, hungering, thirsting, sleeping, weeping, because he was the Son of God; and the Bible, with all its marks of human

---

[2] Commentary on Genesis. By James S. Murphy, LL.D.

hands and human weaknesses, is none the less a revelation of the word and will of God. Says Dr. Schaff, in his "Ancient Christianity:" "The New Testament presents in its way the same union of the divine and human natures as the person of Christ. In this sense also the 'word is made flesh and dwells among us.' The Bible is thoroughly human (though without error) in contents and form, in the mode of its rise, its compilation, its preservation, and transmission; yet at the same time thoroughly divine both in its thoughts and words, in its origin, vitality, energy, and effect, and beneath the human servant-form of the letter the eye of faith discerns the glory of the only-begotten of the Father, full of grace and truth." [3]

<small>Dr. Schaff on likeness of Scripture to Christ's person.</small>

Westcott says, in his "Introduction to the Study of the New Testament:" "The human powers of the divine messenger act according to their natural laws, even when these laws are supernaturally strengthened. Man is not converted into a mere machine even in the hand of God.... The nature of man is not neutralized by the divine agency, and the truth of God is not impaired, but exactly expressed in one of its several aspects to the individual mind."

<small>Westcott on Inspiration.</small>

If the inspiration were verbal, then a constant miracle would have been required from the beginning to preserve the purity of the text, and every transcriber and translator into a new language must necessarily enjoy the same inspiration from the Holy Spirit.[4]

<small>Verbal Inspiration would require a constant miracle.</small>

[3] History of the Christian Church, vol. i, p. 93.

[4] Dean Milman presents this objection to what is sometimes called *mechanical* or verbal inspiration. "Is it the Hebrew or the Greek Septuagint of which

But the Holy Spirit has simply acted *through* men, with divine wisdom revealing its own truths, while they have expressed it in accordance with their natural constitution and abilities. Through all Scripture Christ, the word of God, speaks from first to last, and all Scripture is permanently fitted for our instruction; "a true spiritual meaning, eternal and absolute, lies beneath historical, ceremonial, and moral details."[4]

The manner in which inspiration is bestowed, like every other gift of God, is determined by the necessities of the case. "At one time we may picture to ourselves the lawgiver recording the letter of the divine law which he had received directly from God 'inscribed

Illustration of the varied forms of inspiration.

---

every sentence, phrase, word, syllable is thus inspired. Every one knows, or ought to know, how much they differ, not only in the sense, but in omissions and additional passages found in one, not in the other. It will be said, of course, the Hebrew. But the writers of the New Testament, when their citations are verbally accurate, usually quote the Septuagint. For three or four centuries till the time of Jerome, the Septuagint was the Old Testament of the Church. Till Jerome no one of the Christian fathers, except perhaps Origen, knew Hebrew. All this time, then, the Christian world was without the true, genuine, only-inspired Scripture. For above ten centuries more the Church was dependent on the fidelity and Hebrew knowledge of Jerome for the inspired word of God. Luther must have been, in this view, a greater benefactor to mankind than his fondest admirers suppose by his appeal to the Hebrew original, and was Luther an infallible authority for every word and syllable?"—*Preface to History of the Jews*, p. 43.

"What matters it," says St. Augustine in commenting upon the passage, "Save, Lord, we perish," the words and the time of their utterance being variously reported by the evangelists; "What matters it whether the disciples, in calling on the Lord, really used one or another of these expressions, or some other differing from them all, but still giving the sense that they were perishing, and called on him to save them?"—*How to Study the New Testament*, Dean Alford, p. 20.

[4] Westcott, p. 444.

upon tables of stone' or spoken 'face to face.' At another we may watch the sacred historian, unconsciously it may be, and yet freely, seizing on those facts in the history of the past which were the turning-points of a nation's spiritual progress, gathering the details which combine to give the truest picture of each crisis, and grouping all according to the laws of a marvelous symmetry, which in after-times might symbolize their hidden meaning. Or we may see the prophet gazing intently on the great struggle going on around him, discerning the spirits of men and the springs of national life, till the relations of time no longer exist in his vision—till all strife is referred to the final conflict of good and evil foreshadowed in the great judgments of the world, and all hope is centered in the coming of the Saviour and in the certainty of his future triumph. Another, perhaps, looks within his own heart, and as a new light is poured over its inmost depths, his devotion finds expression in songs of personal penitence and thanksgiving, in confession of sin and declarations of righteousness, which go far to reconcile the mysterious contradictions of our nature. To another is given the task of building up the Church. By divine instinct he sees in scattered congregations types of the great forms of society in coming ages, and addresses to them, not systems of doctrine, but doctrine embodied in deed, which applies to all time, because it expresses eternal truths, and yet specially to each time, because it is connected with the realities of daily life." [6]

Thus all the different Scripture writings taken together

[6] Introduction to the Study of the Gospels, Westcott, p. 37.

may be considered one harmonious message of God spoken in many parts and many manners, *by* men and *to* men, the distinct lessons of individual ages reaching from one time to all time.

This same idea of inspiration is expressed by Alford in the prolegomena to his edition of the Greek Testament. He says, "The inspiration of the sacred writers I believe to have consisted in the fullness of the influence of the Holy Spirit specially raising them to, and enabling them for, their work, in a manner which distinguishes them from all other writers in the world, and their work from all other works. The men were full of the Holy Ghost; the books are the pouring out of that fullness through the men, the conservation of the treasure in earthern vessels. The treasure is ours in all its richness; but it is ours as only it can be ours, in the imperfections of human speech, in the limitations of human thought, in the variety incident at first to individual character, and then to manifold transcription and the lapse of ages. The men were inspired, and the books are the results of that inspiration." [6]

Alford on inspiration.

[6] Prolegomena to Alford's Greek Testament, Harper's Edition, p. 21. With the exception of the clause in the following quotation, which is italicized, we could not find, perhaps, a better succinct presentation of the doctrine of inspiration than is given by Garbett in his able treatise, written chiefly in defense of the theory of verbal inspiration. The author does not adhere to his definition in the body of his work. "There was (in writing the Holy Scriptures) a concurrence of the act of God with the act of man. First, he endowed the man with these particular gifts, and chose him to be his instrument. Secondly, he guided his mind in the selection of what he should say, and of the revelation of the material of his writing where such a revelation was made necessary through the defect of human knowledge. Thirdly, he acted in and on the intellect and

Professor Murphy, in his introduction, presents the view which the Scriptures themselves take of the nature of their own inspiration, insisting, like Gaussen, upon the inspiration of the book rather than of the writers. The Bible, however, just as clearly affirms that the holy men who wrote it were "moved by the Holy Ghost" as that the pages they inscribed were inspired. "The Apostle Paul," says Professor Murphy, "in writing to Timothy, a pastor and teacher in the Church of God, makes use of the following expressions (literally rendered) concerning Scripture: 'The holy *Scripta*, able to make thee wise unto salvation;' and, 'Every Scripture given by inspiration of God and profitable for doctrine.' From these expressions we gather the following order of doctrine concerning the origin and character of the Bible: 1. It is given by inspiration of God. 2. It is first holy; second, able to make wise unto salvation; and third, profitable for doctrine and other purposes of edification. In these elements of the doctrine of inspiration the following points are worthy of remark: 1. It is a *writing*, not a writer, of which the character is here given. The thing said to be inspired is not that which goes into the mind of the author, but that which comes out of his mind by means of his pen. It is not the material on which he is

The Scripture view of inspiration.

heart of the writer in the act of committing the words to writing; not only bestowing a more than human elevation, but securing the truthfulness of the thing written, and *moulding the language into the form accordant to his own will*. To sum up the whole, verbal inspiration simply amounts to this: that while the words of Scripture are truly and characteristically the words of men, they are at the same time fully and concurrently the words of God."—*God's Word Written*, p. 358. We should rather say, in the last clause of the closing sentence, *they* (the words) *do fully and concurrently reveal the will of God.*

to exercise his mind, but the result of that mental exercise which is here characterized. Hence, it has received all the impress, not merely of man in general, but even of the individual author in particular, at the time when it is so designated. It is that piece of composition which the human author has put into a written form which is described as inspired. 2. To be inspired of God, is to be communicated from God, who is a Spirit, to the mind of man. The mode of communication we do not pretend to explain, but the possibility of such communication we cannot for a moment doubt. The immediate author of a human book may not be the ultimate author of a single sentiment it contains. He may have received every fact from trustworthy witnesses, who are, after all, the real vouchers for all it records; and the very merit of the immediate author may consist in judiciously selecting the facts, faithfully adhering to his authorities, and properly arranging his materials for the desired effect. Analogous to this is the divine authorship of the sacred volume. By the inspiration of the Almighty the human author is made to perceive certain things divine and human, to select such as are to be revealed, and to record these with fidelity in the natural order, and to the proper end. The result is a writing given by inspiration of God, with all the peculiarities of man and all the authority of God. 3. Such a written revelation is 'holy.' The primary holiness of a writing is its *truth.* God's part in it secures its veracity and credibility. Even man often tells the truth where he is a disinterested witness; and we believe not only his sincerity

[margin: Illustration of the double authorship of the Bible.]

[margin: The holiness of the Bible.]

but his competence. God, who cannot lie, is able to secure his scribes from error, intentional or unintentional. The secondary holiness of a writing appears in the two following particulars: 4. It is also 'able to make wise unto salvation.'

<small>Office of the Bible.</small> This refers to the kind of truth contained in the book of God. It is a revelation of mercy, of peace on earth, and good-will to man. This, at the same time, imparts an unspeakable interest to the book, and points out the occasion warranting the divine interference for its composition. 5. It is also 'profitable for doctrine.' It tends to holiness. It is moral as well as merciful in its revelations. It contains truth, mercy, and righteousness. It reflects, therefore, the holiness of God. It is in all respects worthy of its high original."[7]

The discussion upon this vital topic may be closed by <small>Summary of discussion.</small> saying that this completed book of holy writings has, from its beginning to its end, been prepared under the immediate direction and inspiration of the divine Spirit, and through all its various pages God does disclose his nature and perfections to our race, and so exhibits his purposes of mercy to mankind that whoever earnestly, prayerfully, and with a penitent heart, searches them will be made by them "wise unto salvation."

[7] Commentary on Genesis, by J. G. Murphy, LL.D., p. 12.

CHAPTER III.

THE CANON: ITS GENUINENESS.

HOW natural the question, as we open our English Bibles: "If the first portions of this volume were written more than twenty-three hundred years ago, and the last book nearly eighteen hundred years since, how strong a confidence may I place in our version, that in it we have, with great exactness, the revelations of the Holy Spirit as they were inspired and recorded by the holy men who received them?" <small>Is our English Bible the word of God as revealed?</small>

The Old Testament was nearly all of it written in Hebrew. The portions composed during and after the captivity of the Jews in Babylon were written in a dialect very similar, and called after the nations from whom they learned it, the Chaldee. <small>Original language of Old Testament.</small>

The canon of the Old Testament—so called from the Greek word κανών, a cane, a measure, a perfect rule—as containing the full and divine measure of inspiration and perfect rule of faith and life, was completed about four hundred years before Christ. Ezra is supposed carefully to have gathered together the sacred books written before his day after the return from the captivity. His own record, and that of Nehemiah, were afterward added, and no further addition was made. <small>The canon.</small>

Certain interesting historical books, recounting the wars of the Jews under the Maccabean princes between the closing of the canon and the times of Christ, stretching over a period B. C. 325 to B. C. 160, together with certain other books of poetry, proverbs, personal incidents, and improbable fables, under the title of Apocrypha, were formerly bound up in the volume with the sacred canon. These books are only of value for the light they throw upon this period of Jewish history, and the evidence, by striking contrast, in almost every respect, which they give of the inspiration of the other Scriptures. The Jews never accounted them to be a part of the holy writings, and it was left to the Roman Church, at the council held in 1546 in Trent in Austria, composed chiefly of Italian cardinals and bishops, called together by the pope, to put " for the first time the apocryphal books in the rank of the Scriptures of God."[1]

Apocrypha.

Value of these books.

How they found a place in the Bible.

There is evidence in the Hebrew Scriptures themselves, in their constant reference to the law of God as contained in preceding holy writings, the public reading of them, and general regard for them, of the extraordinary care taken for their preservation, and for the purity of their transcription.

Care taken of Jewish Scriptures.

The books of the law were placed in the tabernacle with the ark of the covenant, and were kept there during the journeys in the wilderness, and afterward in the Land of Promise.[2] To the same sanctuary were the various historical, poetical, and prophetical books consigned. On the erection of the

---

[1] The Canon of Scripture, by Gaussen, p. 454.
[2] Deut. xxxi, 9, 26; 1 Sam. x, 25; 2 Kings xxii, 8; Isa. xxxiv, 16.

temple Solomon deposited in it these sacred treasures, and enriched them by inspired productions from his own pen. What became of the sacred books when the temple was destroyed we are not informed, but in Babylon Daniel speaks of the book of the law as familiar to him, and also of the prophets.[3]

Bible in Babylon.

Jewish writers, like Philo, the Alexandrine Jew, born thirty years before Christ, and Josephus, in Christ's time, unite in declaring the general correctness of the text in their day; and we may readily believe, after admitting the inspiration of the volume, that the Providence of the same Divine Spirit that supervised its records and gave its revelations would secure its preservation.

Philo and Josephus.

Reason to expect its preservation.

Additional grounds of confidence are found in the fact that about the time of the close of the canon (B. C. 400) a copy of the five books of Moses was made in the Samaritan dialect, for that singular people, a mixture of Hebrews and Chaldeans, gathered in that portion of the land of Israel called Samaria in Christ's times, during the captivity. These sacred writings this people (who kept up their separate life and their enmity for the Jewish people, an enmity which was as earnestly returned by them) as carefully preserved as their Hebrew neighbors did their copies. In A. D. 1623 a full copy of the Samaritan Pentateuch was obtained from a body of this nation in Damascus by De Saucy, the French embassador at Constantinople. Other copies have since been obtained from the East, and the text

Samaritan Pentateuch.

[3] Daniel ix, 2, 11.

of the two versions have been carefully compared, showing a remarkable correspondence.

About three hundred years before Christ, through the Macedonian invasion of Syria and Persia by Alexander the Great, the Greek language and literature were spread over these countries. Alexander built a renowned city, bearing his name, upon the Mediterranean in Egypt. During the wars resulting in the Chaldean captivity many of the Jews had removed to Egypt; more followed under the persecutions of Antiochus, the successor of Alexander in the government of Syria. Ptolemy, and his successors who bore his name, into whose hands Egypt fell upon the great conqueror's death, were generous in their treatment of their Jewish subjects, and encouraged their emigration to the ancient land of their former bondage. They had a temple in Leontopolis similar to the temple at Jerusalem, and followed the Mosaic order in their worship. These Jews all used the Greek language. About the year two hundred and eighty before Christ, for the benefit of these Hellenistic or Grecian Jews at Alexandria, or at the suggestion of Demetrius Phalerius, librarian of the world-renowned royal library at Alexandria, a Greek version of the Hebrew Bible was made. This was called the Septuagint, that is, Seventy, from the tradition that seventy persons were employed in its execution. Many unreliable fables are related of its origin. The translators may have been appointed by the Sanhedrim, or Council of Seventy, at Jerusalem, or their work may have been authenticated by the council consisting of the same number at Alexandria.

This version is a very free and not always exact translation of the Hebrew Scriptures, but is interesting and important as the most ancient version of the entire Old Testament, and as made by learned Jews at a period long before the date of the oldest existing Hebrew manuscripts, and before the Christian era. *Value of this version.* However widely Jews and Christians now differ from each other in their views of the Messiah, both receive as the word of their common Lord and Master this embodied and completed canon of ancient Scripture.

But still more interesting and important is the fact that it was this version of the Old Testament which was used by our Lord and his apostles, and *This version used by our Lord.* from which they made the many hundred quotations to be found throughout the pages of the New Testament. This version renders valuable service in the establishment of the correctness of the present text, and in the elucidation of the meaning of the Hebrew Scriptures.

Having passed the supervision of the Son of God, and having been given afresh by him to the world as the Scriptures of truth, and affirmed to be full of disclosures of himself and his kingdom,[*] the question as to whether we have the whole revelation of God, and with a good degree of correctness, as to the Old Testament, is most satisfactorily answered. The books in this version are the same found in our English Bibles.

[*] John v, 39; Luke xxiv, 27, 44.

Since the death of Christ the noted Rabbinical schools in Palestine and in the further East, and Jewish scholars of various nations, have united with Christians in seeking to perpetuate pure copies of these venerable Scriptures, which contain the foundations of their common faith.

<small>Rabbinical schools.</small>

For the benefit of Christians who had fled to the East in the persecutions that followed the death of Christ, a version of the Old and New Testaments in the first century was made in the ancient Syriac or Aramaic dialect, the tongue generally spoken by the Jews in Palestine in the days of our Lord, and which he himself used. This version is called the Peshito. An ancient tradition, which is considered at least to be probable, says that this version was made by translators who were evidently Jewish Christians, and who were sent from the city of Edesa, in Persia, by the apostle Jude, at the instance of King Abgarus. This version is of great critical value. Several ancient Arabic versions and the Persian version of the Gospels were made from it.

<small>The Syriac or Peshito version.</small>

There were several Latin versions of the Bible made from the Septuagint, the most valuable of which was called the Italic, made, it is believed, in the first century from Alexandrian manuscripts. This version was highly esteemed by Augustine, who died in the year of our Lord four hundred and thirty.

<small>Italic version.</small>

Origen was one of the most learned, as he was the most famous, of the early fathers. He was born in Alexandria A. D. one hundred and eighty-five. He wrote voluminous commentaries upon all the books of

<small>Origen and his version.</small>

Scripture; but his great work was the thorough revision which he made of the Septuagint. He collated it with the original Hebrew, and as many Greek and other versions as he could secure. He spent twenty-eight years upon this work, and traveled throughout the East collecting materials for it. This vast work, which consisted of six parallel versions, and of some books eight, extended to fifty volumes; only portions of it, however, were transcribed, and have been preserved, while the main work perished. The result of his studies in correcting the Septuagint were not entirely lost.

Jerome, the most learned of the early European fathers, was born in the province of Dalmatia, now in the empire of modern Austria, A. D. 346. He studied at Rome, and in the German city Treves. Afterward for four years he devoted himself to the study of the Scriptures in a cell near the city of Antioch in Asia Minor. Here he acquired that skill in the Hebrew language which he turned to so good account. At this time the manuscript copies of the Latin versions of the Bible had become very corrupt through omissions and additions, notes and comments being often given as a portion of the sacred text. Jerome was highly esteemed for his scholarship and saintly character by Damasus, Bishop of Rome, and at his request was induced to undertake a new version of the Bible in Latin, then the prevailing language of the Western or European Church. He availed himself of the labors of Origen, and of all the early Eastern versions of the Scriptures. Being dissatisfied with the Septuagint translation of the Hebrew Bible he made a new version from the Hebrew text. This version surpasses all former

Jerome.

ones in the care with which it is executed, and in its general correctness. This is the famous Vulgate version, (so called because in common use,) still final authority in the Roman Church. It was completed about A. D. 390, but was very slowly and reluctantly allowed to displace other editions in use in the Churches. It was not until the time of Pope Gregory I., in the seventh century, that it met with general acceptance. Its often transcription exposed its text to constant variations, and from time to time new revisions were made. The first book printed was a copy of the Vulgate at Mentz, called the "Mazarin Bible," about A. D. 1455, copies of which are still extant. In 1546 the Council of Trent ordained that this edition should be "esteemed authentic, and that no one should dare to reject it under any pretense whatever." In fact they declared this version to be an inspired book, with no errors in it, although at the same time they tried to correct some of the errors in it.[5]

Pope Sixtus V., in 1590, ordered a revised edition to be issued, corrected himself the proofs, and declared it to be of perpetual authority; but there were so many errors in it that his successor caused the whole edition to be canceled. The work was again undertaken under Clement VIII. and completed in 1592. This is the authoritative edition from which the Roman Catholic copies of the Scriptures in Latin are printed. It is not allowed to be criticised, and is called the Clementine edition.

---

[5] Manuscript notes of Prof. Shedd's Seminary Lectures.

THE WORD OF GOD OPENED. 39

There were other less important early versions, such as the Coptic, the language spoken by the native Egyptians, the Ethiopian, the Gothic, the tongue of the invaders of Rome, Persian, Arabian, etc.; but these that have been described somewhat at length will enable us to see the important service which early transcriptions from these versions afford in the criticism and interpretation of the text of our modern versions of the holy records.

Before referring to this we shall consider the question of the authority and genuineness of the canon of the New Testament. As was stated in the opening chapter, God spake first by inspired men. While the apostles lived and moved about among the Churches the necessity would not exist for a collection of the records of Christ's life and doctrines, or of the instructions of their inspired teachers. The early Christians were permitted to receive the facts of the Gospel from the lips of "eye-witnesses," and to enjoy the discipline of the apostles themselves. *The New Testament canon.* *Inspired men preceded the Scriptures.*

Dr. Whedon remarks, in the introduction to his Commentary upon Luke and John, that after the Gospels had been written, down even to the close of the second century, the early Church clung fondly to the oral traditions handed down from the Saviour's and from apostolical lips. He quotes from Papias as saying: "I do not think that I derived so much benefit from books as from the living voice of those who are still surviving. If I met with any one who had been a follower of the elders (the apostles and their contemporaries) I made it a point *Dr. Whedon on oral communications from the apostolical age.*

to inquire what were the declarations of the elders, and what was said by Andrew, Peter, or Philip; what by Thomas, James, John, Matthew, or any of the disciples of our Lord." The quotation shows both that sacred manuscripts were then in existence, and also that their personal traditions from the lips of the apostles corresponded with them and confirmed them. In a day when books could only be multiplied by the painful process of copying letter for letter, we can readily see how precious these personal oral discourses must have been. It would appear probable that at an early day many persons made records of such incidents and discourses of our Lord as came to their hearing, for Luke says in the introduction to his Gospel: "Forasmuch as *many* have taken in hand to *set forth in order* a declaration of those things which are most surely believed among us, even as they delivered them unto us, which from the beginning were eye-witnesses, and ministers of the word; it seemed good to me also, having had perfect understanding *of all things from the very first*, to write," etc.

Many records made.

The fact that all these other written records were allowed to perish, and are never referred to or quoted by early Christian writers, is a very significant evidence of the different estimation in which the four evangelical records were held, and of the satisfactory character of the writings that have been thus divinely preserved amid the general loss of all other histories of these amazing facts.

All these records disappeared.

The Gospels were universally admitted in the early Church to have been written by the persons whose names they bear,

Matthew, who remained in Jerusalem, wrote his Gospel first, primarily for the benefit of the Hebrew Christians that remained through all the persecutions in Judea. He is thought by some to have been related to the apostle James, sometimes called the head of the Church in Jerusalem,[6] and a similarity is pointed out between Matthew's record of the Sermon upon the Mount and the Epistle of James. He brings out before his Jewish readers with great distinctness the Messiahship of Jesus, his true kingly character, and his office as sent to the lost sheep of the house of Israel. From James, who was, after the flesh, a kinsman of the Lord, he may have learned "the mystery of that birth, the genealogy of inheritance which heirs of the house of David treasured up, the visit of the wise men, the flight into Egypt. How such a record met the cravings of human hearts we may judge from the hold which the history of the nativity has in all ages had upon countless thousands of loving and childlike hearts."[7]

Matthew wrote for the Jewish Christians.

Presents the Messiahship and kingly character of Christ.

"The Gospel of St. Matthew," says Alford, "is that one to which we owe, more than to any other, our complete idea of our blessed Lord as the promised Messiah, the holy one of God, the king and head over all to his Church. In the vivid depictions of St. Mark we have ever his personal image before us, and the very sound of his voice; in the careful and precious collections of St. Luke we see him as the Saviour of our race, the head and root of our humanity; while it is from this first and best known of the Gospels that the image of

[6] Christ and Christendom, pp. 53–56. [7] Ibid.

him especially arises, which is so much in the thoughts and hearts of all of us who believe—that chosen One, in whom center all the ways and works of God; perfect in majesty, perfect in mercy; the king's son, for whom is made the great marriage of heaven and earth; the bridegroom, into whose feast the wise and virgin souls shall enter; the king himself, who shall come to take account of his own servants; nay, who shall come, and all the holy angels with him, and sit on the throne of his glory, with all the nations before him, and allot to every one his eternal doom." [8]

Mark.

John, surnamed Mark, was the nephew of Barnabas.[9] His mother, the sister of Paul's first companion in missionary labors,[10] must have been an early disciple, and her house in Jerusalem the resort, perhaps, of Christ and the apostles. Certainly Peter made a home there.[11] The old tradition is strongly confirmed that he wrote his Gospel under the guidance of the apostle Peter. He was with this apostle when he wrote his epistles to the Churches.[12] In the Second Epistle Peter intimates that he had taken measures to enable the Asiatic Churches to "have in remembrance" that the incidents which they had heard about the Lord Jesus Christ from his lips were not "cunningly-devised fables."[13] Probably in this he referred to the fact that his son Marcus, as he affectionately calls him, was recording from his lips the incidents in sacred history that had passed under his eye Of his Gospel, Plumptre remarks, "There are, as has been

Written under sanction of Peter.

Peter seems to promise a Gospel.

---

[8] How to Study the New Testament, p. 77. [9] Acts iv, 36. [10] Acts xiii, 2
[11] Acts xii, 12. [12] 1 Peter v, 13. [13] 2 Peter i, 15, 16.

often noticed, vivid pictorial touches which speak of knowledge such as belongs to an eye-witness: The scene of the 'green grass' in Bethsaida, and the groups in which the multitude arranged themselves by hundreds and fifties; the dashing of the waves in the ship while our Lord was sleeping on the boat's cushion in the stern; the smaller craft that accompanied the ship of the disciples; the touches of personal knowledge in the history of the demoniac who plucked asunder his chains and ground his fetters together till they were broken; of the woman with the issue of blood, who had suffered many things of many physicians, and had spent all that she had;[14] of the glance and gesture with which the Lord looked round in anger at the hardness of men's hearts, or in pity and yearning love upon the rich young ruler, or in approving welcome to the disciples whom he claimed as his true kindred; the special notice of the strange apparition in Gethsemane of the young man with the linen cloth cast around his naked body;[15] these are but a few of the long list of details of like nature." *Evidently written by an eye-witness.*

Mark's Gospel is not eminently one adapted for the Hebrews like Matthew's, nor for the Gentiles as was Luke's, but belonged equally to both, as Peter was at once an apostle to the circumcision, and was chosen to open the door of faith to the Gentile world.[16] *Adapted to Jew and Gentile.*

Luke, the "beloved physician"[17] and companion of Paul, is supposed to have written the two treat- *Luke.*

---

[14] Mark iv, 36, 38; v, 25, 26; vi, 39, 40.
[15] Mark iii, 5; x, 21; iii, 34.
[16] Christ and Christendom, p. 49.
[17] Colossians iv, 14.

ises bearing his name under the eye of the apostle to the Gentiles. Luke is supposed to have been a resident of Antioch, and to have become acquainted with Paul in this city.[18] This city became the center of the Gentile Church, as Jerusalem was of the Church of the circumcision. "The prominence given to the arrival there of the men of wider thoughts who left Jerusalem after the death of Stephen, and then of the men of Cyprus and Cyrene, who took the bold step of preaching to the heathen, and then of Barnabas and Saul, the stress laid on the new name of Christian, as originating there, and on the liberality of that Church to the poor at Jerusalem; the list of prophets conspicuous there; but, with the exception of Paul and Barnabas, not otherwise memorable,[19] are all indications of the writer's residence in Antioch between the time of St. Paul's conversion and his first missionary journey. And if so, then we are able to trace, with hardly a shadow of uncertainty, the channels through which he may have obtained most of the materials of his narrative. Those that fled from Jerusalem on the persecution must have included some of the personal disciples of Christ.[20] The fullness with which all facts connected with the personal history of Herod Antipas are told is accounted for when we remember that one of the chief teachers at Antioch was Manaen, the foster

Antioch.

The sources of Luke's Gospel.

---

[18] "Luke, the beloved physician, and Demas, greet you." Thus wrote St. Paul from his prison at Rome to the Colossians. "Demas hath forsaken me having loved this present world. . . . Only Luke is with me." Thus he wrote some years after when he was now ready to be offered up, and the time of his departure was at hand, to his *son* Timotheus.—*Dean Alford*.

[19] Acts xiii, 1.   [20] Acts xxi, 16.

THE WORD OF GOD OPENED. 45

brother of the tetrarch; that the wife of Herod's steward had been one of the faithful women who followed our Lord through his ministrations. The clew thus obtained leads us, I believe, yet farther. 1. One of the most distinctive features of the Gospel of St. Luke is the full collection of parables and narratives, belonging all of them to one and the same journey, the last journey through Peræa toward Jerusalem. In Peræa was one of the strongholds of Antipas. If there were those in his court who were avowedly or in heart disciples of the Nazarene, this would be the teaching with which they would come most in contact, and be most anxious to preserve. 2. Hardly less characteristic is the special fullness and the marked Hebrew stamp of his narrative of the nativity. Was he incorporating a Hebrew record with his own? and if so, where did that come from? on whose testimony did it rest? why was it preserved? Friendship with Herod's foster-brother and the wife of Herod's steward would lead to some knowledge of the other members of the devout circle of women whom St. Luke names so conspicuously,[21] of the mother of James and John, of Mary of Magdala, of those sisters of Bethany whom he is the first to mention.[22] But in that group there had once been one around whom they must have gathered with the love of daughters, and all but the reverential awe of worshipers. They had known the mother of the Lord. Some of them must have lived for years in closest contact with her. They would treasure up every record of that marvelous history which she had kept and

Parables of Luke.

Account of the nativity.

[21] Luke viii, 2, 3.   [22] Luke x, 38 42.

pondered in her heart. From them and through them, with no doubtful or deteriorating transmission, from her may have come that which we may call the true Gospel of the infancy."[23]

John outlived all the apostles, and is recorded to have ac-

John knowledged publicly the authority of the first three Gospels, and to have added his own to complete them. In the same way, though less directly, he is supposed to have attested the book of Acts.[24] "As there were rea sons," Plumptre remarks in his lectures, from which we have already quoted, "personal, it may be, which prevented the record of the raising of Lazarus from being made known till

Early Gospels reserved on some points. he himself had died or had left Jerusalem, so, as long as the apostle remained there, in filial con- secration of his life to the care of his Lord's mother, the records that were current in the Churches of Palestine were probably in harmony with that reserve, and are represented by what reflects directly and indirectly the teaching of the apostles of the circumcision, modified in the case of Luke by his association with St. Paul and with the prophets of An- tioch, and in that of St. Mark by his fellowship with both St. Peter and St. Paul, the substance, that is, of the first three Gospels. But when the changes of his life carried the fisher- man of Bethsaida to the Asiatic Churches he found the way

Paul had opened the way for his Gospel. prepared for him by the labors of the apostle of the Gentiles. The Gospel, communicated at Je- rusalem privately, and to a few, had been preached in its

---

[23] Christ and Christendom, pp. 64, 68.
[24] Wordsworth on the Canon, pp. 156, 160.

fullness to those to whom that apostle had not shrunk (manifestly contrasting himself with other teachers who did shrink) from 'proclaiming the whole counsel of God;' to whom he had spoken of the blood shed upon the cross as the blood of God;[25] who had heard, in the utterance of prophets, that God, or Christ as the Son of God, had been manifest in the flesh;[26] that in him dwelt the fullness of the Godhead bodily.[27] Side by side with this preparation for the truth there were strange caricatures and denials of it. Some denied that the Christ had come in the flesh,[28] others that Jesus was the Christ,[29] or that he was indeed the Son of God,[30] or that they had any fellowship with him, and through him with the Father. For them the Christ was a Jewish teacher only, or all true personality was lost in dreams and words. Here, then, was that which called for something more than the Church already had—for the witness, which none could bear so well as the disciple whom Jesus loved, to the reality of his Lord's human nature, his affection, his weariness, his tears—to what had been his own teaching as to himself and his relation to his Father, when that teaching reached its highest point and revealed the full glory of the truth. It might seem at first that the tie of a divine adoption, which brought together St. John and the mother of the Lord, would have led him to give with a rich and overflowing fullness a record of the facts of the nativity, instead of leaving it in a profound silence; yet the very omission is, I believe,

False views of Christ.

John presents the true idea.

Why he says nothing of the nativity.

[25] Acts xx. 28. [26] 1 Tim. iii. 16. [27] Col. i. 19.
[28] 1 John iv. 3. [29] 1 John ii. 22. [30] 1 John iv. 15.

significant and instructive. The record of all that Christians needed as to that history was current already in the Church. In the very depths of his sympathy and reverence for the virgin mother his spirit would grow like hers, who 'kept all these things, and pondered them in her heart.' A Church in which that history occupies in men's minds a position out of proportion to that which is assigned to it in the Gospel record, is on its way to Mariolatry. With an anticipation, conscious or unconscious, of the dangers of a time to come,

<small>John gives the strong meat of the Gospel.</small> St. John, leaving others to give the "pure milk" which was needed for the life of spiritual childhood, himself supplies the "strong meat," the solid food of thought, meeting the wants of those who are of full age—the cravings of man's heart and reason. If he names the mother of the Lord, whom he had known so well, it is to indicate in what entire independence of her control and guidance he had manifested his kingdom,[31] not as exalted to a throne left vacant in the heavens, a title wonderful and majestic, but as a mother, lonely and bereaved, needing the protection which it had been his duty and joy to give."

Dr. Barnes, in his course of lectures upon the "Evidences of Christianity," remarking upon the humble origin, as compared with the influence of their writings, of the inspired authors, refers to the Apostle John as an illustration, and goes on to say: "He was a fisherman on the Lake of Tiberias when Jesus first saw him and called him to the work of an apostle. We have his Gospel, and we have his book of 'Revelation,' and, bearing in remembrance that he was a

<small>[31] John ii, 4.</small>

fisherman, we are to ask, What would *fishermen* taken from the banks of the Delaware, from Marblehead and Gloucester, or from the Banks of Newfoundland, be likely to produce if called to compose a book on the subject of John's Gospel or the Book of Revelation?" Dr. Barnes proceeds to quote from a discourse of Dr. Dwight, in which the same thought is eloquently developed: "The apostle John was born in an age when the philosophy of his country was a mere mass of quibbling, its religion a compound of pride and bigotry, and its worship a ceremonious parade. His lineage, his circumstances, and his employment were those of a fisherman. On what natural principle can it be accounted for that, like the sun breaking out of an evening cloud, this plain man, in these circumstances, should at an advanced age burst upon mankind with a flood of effulgence and glory? Whence did it arise that in purity of precept, discernment of truth, and an acquaintance with the moral character of man and the attributes of his Maker, this peasant leaves Socrates, Plato, and Cicero out of sight and out of remembrance? Do you question the truth of this representation? The proof is at hand and complete. There is not a child of fifteen who, if possessed of the common education of this land, would not disdain to worship *their* gods or to embrace *their* religion. But Bacon and Boyle, Butler and Berkeley, Newton and Locke, Addison and Johnson, Jones and Horsley, have submissively embraced the religion of St. John, and worshiped the God whose character he has unfolded. *Their* systems have long since gone to the grave of oblivion. *His* has been animated with increasing

Literature of St. John the fisherman.

vigor to the present hour, and will live and flourish through endless ages. *Their* writings have not made one man virtuous. *His* have peopled heaven with the children of light. The seventeenth chapter of his Gospel, written as it is with the simplicity of a child, in grandeur of conception and in splendor of moral excellence triumphs with inexpressible glory over all the efforts of human genius, and looks down from heaven on the proudest labors of infidelity." [32]

There are thirteen of the epistles of Paul which bear his name. His companions, Christian ministers, were his amanuenses, or witnessed his writing these letters.[33] His epistles were sent to the Churches by private messengers.[34] Nine of them were addressed to public bodies, and he commanded them to be openly read.

<small>Paul and his epistles.</small>

Peter, in his epistle, bears witness to the fact that they were accounted as inspired Scriptures,[35] and read with those of the Old Testament. Indeed, when Peter wrote his epistles, all the epistles of Paul had been written, and are, therefore, referred to under this title of Scriptures, a term only applied by the Jews to inspired writings. "The conclusion, therefore, is, that these epistles are Paul's, (whose name they bear,) and that they have what Paul claimed for them, and what the early Church ascribed to them, inspired, and therefore canonical, authority. They are not the words which man teaches; they are the words of the Holy Ghost."

<small>Peter bears his testimony to their inspired authority.</small>

---

[32] Quoted in Evidences of Christianity in the Nineteenth Century, p. 259.
[33] 1 Thess. i, 1; 2 Thess. i, 1; Rom. xvi, 22.
[34] Romans xvi, 1.   [35] 2 Peter iii, 15, 16.

THE WORD OF GOD OPENED. 51

The apostle who survived the others, the beloved John, died at the close of the first century. Within the period of a human life after his death Papias, bishop of Hierapolis, in Asia Minor, about A. D. 120, and Irenæus, born about A. D. 140, and who died at the beginning of the next century, professing to record the testimony of the generation before them, refer to the Gospels as we have them, as "the words or oracles of the Lord."[36] Irenæus was bishop of the first Christian Church at Lyons in Gaul, now France. He wrote a great work against the errorists of the day, and quoted from the Gospels, as admitted by all to be final authority. He quotes about four hundred passages from them. He also quoted from all the epistles, except Philemon and Hebrews, of which Dr. Lardner, in his work upon the "Credibility of the Scriptures," gives eighteen examples. Irenæus,[37] in his youth, sat at the feet of the aged Polycarp,

Papias and Irenæus.

---

[36] Christ and Christendom, by E. H. Plumptre, p. 41.

[37] Westcott remarks in his "History of the Canon of the New Testament," "It is almost impossible for any one whose ideas of communication are suggested by the railway and the printing-press to understand how far mere material hinderances must have prevented a speedy and unanimous settlement of the canon. The means of intercourse were slow and precarious. The multiplication of manuscripts in remote provinces was tedious and costly. The common meeting-point of Christians was destroyed by the fall of Jerusalem, and from that time national Churches grew up around their separate centers, enjoying in a great measure the freedom of individual development, and exhibiting, often in exaggerated forms, peculiar tendencies of doctrine or ritual. As a natural consequence, the circulation of different parts of the New Testament for a while depended more or less on their supposed connection with specific forms of Christianity." After illustrating this statement, he goes on to say, "From the close of the second century the history of the canon is simple, and its proof is clear. It is allowed even by those who have reduced the genuine apostolic works to the narrowest limits, that from the time of Irenæus the New Testament was composed essentially of the same books which we receive at present"

a disciple of the apostle John. In a letter he thus most affectingly alludes to his acquaintance with this pupil of the apostles: "I can recall the very place where Polycarp used to sit and teach, his manner of speech, his mode of life, his appearance, the style of his address to the people, his frequent reference to St. John and to others who had seen our Lord; how he used to repeat from memory their discourses which he had heard from them concerning our Lord, his miracles and mode of teaching, and how, being instructed himself by those who were eye-witnesses of the Word, there was in all that he said a strict agreement with the Scriptures."[38] What more interesting or satisfactory confirmation could we have than the testimony of this eminent Christian minister, but one generation removed from the apostles, of the estimation, as a divine record, in which our Scriptures of the New Testament were held?

<small>Irenæus a disciple of Polycarp.</small>

The learned and eloquent Tertullian, who lived at Carthage at the close of the second century, makes constant quotations from the Gospels. He says: "We lay this down for a certain truth, that the evangelic Scriptures have for their authors the apostles, to whom the work of publishing the Gospel was committed by the Lord him-

<small>Tertullian.</small>

---

and that they were regarded with the same reverence as is now shown to them." This able scholar then shows, by an exhaustive examination of such writings of the apostolical fathers as still exist, that from the age of the apostles themselves to this period of absolute certainty we have the most assuring testimony, arising out of constant quotations, that the present books of the New Testament came from the hands of the apostles of Christ.

[38] "When were our Gospels written?" Constantine Tischendorf, p. 77.

self. Among the apostles John and Matthew teach us faith, among the apostolical men Luke and Mark refresl it."[39] He speaks with equal respect and positiveness of the epistles: "If you be willing to exercise your curiosity profitably in the business of your salvation visit the apostolical Churches, in which the very chairs of the apostles still preside; in which their very *authentic* letters are recited, sounding forth the voice, and representing the countenance, of each one of them. Is Achaia near you? You have Corinth. If you are not far from Macedonia, you have Philippi, you have Thessalonica. If you can go to Asia you have Ephesus; but if you are near to Italy you have Rome, from whence we may also be easily satisfied."[40]

His testimony as to Gospels and Epistles.

Justin Martyr, who was born not long after the death of the apostles, A. D. 130, and was acquainted with their immediate disciples, speaks often in his writings of the Gospels as of unquestioned authority, under the title of Memoirs of Christ, and says that the "apostles composed them." He also refers to the Acts, to nearly all the epistles, and to the Revelation. He also declares that it was a general practice to read the Gospels "at public worship in Christian assemblies every Lord's day," and to discourse upon them. "We come together," he says, "to recollect the divine Scriptures. We nourish our faith, raise our hope, confirm our trust by the sacred word."[41]

Justin Martyr.

Speaks of use of Scriptures in public assemblies.

---

[39] Canon and Interpretation of the Scriptures, by Professor M'Lelland, p. 56.
[40] Ibid.   [41] Canon and Interpretation, p. 58.

Some time between the first and second century the old Syriac version of the Bible, heretofore referred to, which has come down to us in a sound condition, was made.[42] The most ancient copies of it lacked Second Peter, Second and Third John, and probably James; but with these exceptions it contains all the sacred writings found in the canonical Scriptures, and no other books. The old Italic versions were made in the same period. These contain all the books of our collection.

The Syriac version.

The Italic.

When we come down to the third century we meet the testimony of that unequaled scholar and most faithful stu-

---

[42] Of this version Westcott remarks it "is assigned almost universally to the most remote Christian antiquity. . . . If a conjecture may be allowed, I think that the various facts of the case are adequately explained by supposing that versions of separate books of the New Testament were first made and used in Palestine, perhaps within the apostolic age, and that shortly afterward these were collected, revised, and completed at Edessa. Many circumstances combine to give support to this belief. The early condition of the Syrian Church, its wide extent, and active vigor, lead us to expect that a version of the Holy Scriptures into the common dialect could not have been long deferred; and the existence of an Aramaic Gospel (Matthew) was in itself likely to suggest the work. Differences of style, no less than the very nature of the case, point to separate translations of different books, and at the same time a certain general uniformity of character bespeaks some subsequent revision. I have ventured to specify the place at which I believe that this revision was made. Whatever may be thought of the alleged intercourse of Abgarus, king of Edessa, with our Lord, Edessa itself is signalized in early Church history by many remarkable facts. It was called the 'holy' and the 'blessed' city; its inhabitants were said to have been brought over by Thaddeus in a marvelous manner to the Christian faith, 'and from that time forth' Eusebius adds, 'the whole people of Edessa has continued to be devoted to the name of Christ, exhibiting no ordinary instance of the goodness of our Saviour.' In the second century it became the center of an important Christian school, and long afterward retained its pre-eminence among the cities of its province."—*A General Survey of the History of the Canon of the New Testament.* By BROOKE FOSS WESTCOTT, B. D., p. 206.

dent of the Scriptures for a lifetime, Origen, A. D. 230. He says of the Gospels, as we now accept them, "They are received without dispute by the whole Church of God under heaven." In another place he says, "Matthew sounds first with his priestly trumpet in his Gospel; Mark also, and Luke and John, sounded with their priestly trumpets. Peter likewise sounds aloud with the two trumpets of his epistles, James also, and Jude; and John sounds again with his trumpet in his epistles and the Revelation, and Luke also, once more relating the actions of the apostles. Last of all (in his list of books) comes Paul, and, sounding with the trumpet of his fourteen epistles, he threw down to the foundations the walls of Jericho, and all the engines of idolatry, and the schemes of the philosophers." [43]

Origen on the New Testament.

About the year A. D. 300 a learned, wealthy, and Christian minister and book collector named Pamphilus gathered every scrap of Christian literature upon which he could lay his hands, and upon his death he gave this invaluable library to the Church at Cæsarea in Palestine, where he lived, to be used by Eusebius, his pastor, during his life. He was inflamed with so great a love for sacred literature that he copied with his own hand the chief part of the works of Origen. His library is frequently mentioned by ancient writers. Jerome found the works of Origen in this library. Out of this large and rare material Eusebius wrote his history of the Church during the preceding centuries, and authenticates the in-

Pamphilus.

Eusebius.

[43] Canon and Interpretation, p. 55.

spired books which had been in use from the beginning. He includes all found in our present canon, and no others.

Constantine the Great, the Roman emperor, who was the contemporary of the Bishop of Cæsarea, and was an eager and delighted reader of the New Testament, was accustomed to read every day a portion of Scripture to his household, and to offer prayer. He wrote to Eusebius to supervise the preparation for him of fifty copies of the entire Greek Scriptures, and ordered two government wagons, under the special charge of a deacon of the Church at Cæsarea, to transport them when completed to Constantinople. These manuscripts, which Eusebius caused to be executed promptly and with great pleasure, the emperor gave to the principal Churches to be read in the public worship. They were also transcribed for the use of other Churches. To this source, probably, we owe all our best manuscripts of the Greek Testament, the Alexandrian, the Vatican, the Ephraim, and the Sinaitic, discovered by Tischendorf."

Constantine the Great.

Fifty Greek copies of the Scriptures made by Eusebius.

Jerome in the same century, (A. D. 322,) with all the authorities of previous generations under his eye, prepared his well-known Vulgate edition of the Bible, which remains to this day as it came from his hand, save the introduction of the apocryphal books by the Council of Trent.

Jerome.

During the early centuries a few of the books of the New Testament, such as the Epistles of James, Second Peter, and Second and Third John,

Some books of New Testament held a while in suspense.

"Origin and History of the Books of the Bible. By C. E. STOWE, D. D., p 55.

and the Revelation, were for a time held in doubt; but after careful examination were received into the canon. The very hesitation shown both confirms the genuineness of these books (for they were only received after careful examination) and increases our confidence in the divine authority of the others. *Hesitation an evidence of canonicity.* None were received without unqualified apostolical origin. Certain works attributed to the early fathers were sometimes found connected with the inspired manuscripts, as the so-called *Apocryphal New Testament.* "Epistle of Barnabas" and a part of the "Pastor of Hermas" were found united with the Sinaitic manuscript of the Scriptures which Tischendorf found in the convent of Mount Sinai. These writings have never been received by any number of persons as inspired, and are of value only on account of their early Christian origin. In the latter case they show the age of the manuscript with which they were bound, proving it to be one of the oldest *Use of these writings.* copies of the Septuagint, as having been made as early at least as the first half of the fourth century; and by the contrast of their contents they show the unapproachable authority, simplicity, and truth of the divine oracles as gathered into the present canon. The editor of the "Journal of Sacred Literature," B. H. Cooper, has just prepared an edition of the apocryphal Gospels. He says in his introduction, "Before I undertook this work I never realized so completely the impassable character of the gulf which separates the genuine Gospels from these." They originated long after the true Gospels were written, in the second or third century. They consist of idle and unfounded traditions relating to the infancy, youth, and early manhood of our Lord, about which the word of God is silent. They are below contempt. Sacred scholars, from Irenæus down, have denounced them.[45]

The first manuscript version of the whole Bible in the English language was made by John Wiclif A. D. 1380. Its circulation was limited by the great labor and expense of transcribing it, as the art of printing had not yet begun to realize the Pentecostal miracle of tongues, but it was an engine of wonderful power. It was the first morning light ushering in the full day of the Reformation.

<small>First English manuscript of the Bible.</small>

The first printed copy of any portion of the Scriptures in the English tongue was published by William Tyndale about the beginning of the sixteenth century. Unable, through persecution, to accomplish this work at home he went to Germany, and there made his version, not from the Latin Vulgate, as his predecessors had done, but from the original Greek and Hebrew. He issued first the New Testament and afterward the Pentateuch. About the commencement of the

<small>First printed edition of the Bible in English.</small>

<small>William Tyndale.</small>

---

[45] "It is of the utmost importance," says Westcott, "to remember that the canon was never referred in the first ages to the authority of fathers or councils. The appeal was made not to the judgment of men, but to that of Churches, and of those particularly which were most nearly interested in the genuineness of separate writings. And thus it is found that while all the canonical books are supported by the concurrent testimony of all, or at least of many, Churches, no more than isolated opinions of private men can be brought forward in support of the authority of any other writings, for the New Testament Apocrypha can hold a place by the side of the apostolic books only so long as our view is limited to a narrow range. A comprehensive survey of their general relations shows the real interval by which they are separated."—*Canon of N. T.*, p. 449.

year 1535 he was beguiled from the city of Antwerp, where he had found protection, by an English emissary of the Roman Church, and was seized and imprisoned in the castle of Vilvorde, near the city of Brussels. After a wearisome imprisonment, and vain efforts to secure the interposition of the English court, on the 6th of October, 1536, he was led forth to be burned. His last words, "uttered with fervent zeal and in a loud voice, were these: '*Lord, open the king of England's eyes!*'"

Burning of Tyndale.

For ten years he had been an exile from his home, suffering in a foreign land, from poverty and persecution, distresses that only the Christian faith can enable a man to endure, and finally gave his body to be burned, that he might bestow upon all speaking his native tongue the pure written word of God. Such a result, however, was worth all it cost: he "received his reward." "His occupation in this earth," says Froude, "was gone. His eyes saw the salvation for which he had longed, and he might depart to his place."[46]

Soon after Tyndale was thrown into prison an edition of the entire Bible, containing the portions previously published by him, and probably completed from his manuscripts, was commenced by his friend and fellow-exile, John Rogers, and was published in 1537 under the assumed name of Thomas Mathew, and was hence called *Mathew's Bible*. But the editor of it claimed for his friend its authorship by inserting his initials in ornamental letters (W. T.) at the close of the Old Testament. Of the New Testament there could be no doubt as to its origin, as it had

John Rogers publishes his edition of the Bible.

[46] History of England, vol. III, p. 87.

long since been published.[47] The editor discloses himself by appending his initials (J. R.) at the close of a preliminary exhortation to the study of the Holy Scriptures.

So great a change had been produced in influential quarters in England during these memorable years that Lord Cromwell, who was prime minister of England, and also "vicegerent" of King Henry VIII. in all ecclesiastical matters, together with Archbishop Cranmer, persuaded the king, before the first edition of Tyndale's Bible was exhausted, to obtain from Francis I., of France, permission to print an edition of the English Bible in Paris, as the work could be better done there than in England. About the time of Tyndale's imprisonment, according to Froude, but two years later, according to previous authorities, Miles Coverdale, a member of the same Cambridge circle which had given birth to Cranmer, to Latimer, to Barnes, and to the Scotch Wishart, silently went abroad with a license from Cromwell, and, with Tyndale's help, collected and edited the various books of Scripture.[48] As the Inquisition stopped their work in Paris, Cromwell ordered his agents to bring the types and presses, and even the French printers, to England. In 1536, according to Froude, it was published in London, was dedicated to Henry VIII., and the clergy were ordered not only to permit, but to exhort and encourage all men to resort to it and read. "In this act," says the eloquent historian whose dates we have followed, "was laid the foundation-stone on which the whole later

Coverdale's Bible.

---

[47] Popular History of the English Bible, by Mrs. H. C. Conant.
[48] Froude's History of England, vol. iii.

history of England, civil as well as ecclesiastical, has been reared." Of the effect of its publication upon the people, Strype, in his "Life of Cranmer," says, it was a jubilee among the poor of England when, for the first time in the national history, they could listen from Sabbath to Sabbath to "the sweet and glad tidings of the Gospel" without the fear of prisons, the scourge, and the stake. "It was wonderful," he says, "to see with what joy this book of God was received, not only among the learneder sort, and those that were noted for lovers of the Reformation, but generally all England over, among all the vulgar and common people, and with what greediness God's word was read, and what resort to places where the reading of it was. Everybody that could bought the book and busily read it, or got others to read it to them if they could not themselves, and divers more elderly people learned to read on purpose. And even little boys flocked among the rest to hear portions of the Holy Scriptures read." What a blessed preparation was this for the bloody persecutions that afterward tried their faith in God's written word! *Effect of the publication of the Bible.*

Of this version of the Bible Froude says: "Though since that time it has been many times revised and altered, we may say that it is substantially the Bible with which we are all familiar. The peculiar genius—if such a word may be permitted—which breathes through it, the mingled tenderness and majesty, the Saxon simplicity, the preternatural grandeur, unequaled, unapproached in the attempted improvements of modern scholars; all are here, and bear the impress of the mind of one man, William *Froude upon this version.*

Tyndale. Lying while engaged in that great office under the shadow of death, the sword above his head and ready at any moment to fall, he worked under circumstances alone, perhaps, truly worthy of the task which was laid upon him; his spirit, as it were, divorced from the world, moved in a purer element than common air." [40]

By the commencement of the next century numerous editions of the Bible had been made. Even the Romanists, finding that they could not put a stop to the circulation of the Scriptures in the language of the people, felt it necessary to have a version of their own. In 1582 they issued the New Testament at Rheims, and in 1610 the Old Testament at Douay. This forms the famous Douay edition of the Bible, a fine version in some respects, but with its daring changes to meet the requisitions of a fallen Church.

The Douay edition.

Martin Luther, the great German Reformer, who was born in 1483 and died in 1546, has been called the father of modern biblical interpretation, for he taught by precept and example that the Bible in the original tongues is final authority in all religious questions, and that private judgment, and not the decision of councils, is to be allowed to determine its sense. He insisted with characteristic earnestness upon a grammatical and philological mode of interpretation of the language of Scripture, rather than bending the word of God to the preconceived opinions and theories of any religious schools. All the success that has since been secured in the

Martin Luther.

Father of biblical interpretation.

[40] Froude, vol. iii, p. 87.

investigation of the exact meaning of the sacred records has arisen from following the example which he set in this regard. The noblest work of this noble man was the translation of the Scriptures into the German language.[50] The study of the Bible was a life-long passion with him. "Were I but a great poet," he was accustomed to say, "I would write a magnificent poem on the utility and efficacy of the divine word." "His judgment on the different books of the Bible," Westcott remarks, "as given in detail in his prefaces, are so full of life, and so characteristic of the man, that they can never lose their interest; and, as a whole, they form an important chapter in the history of the Bible."[51]

The present version of the English Bible was commenced in 1607 and completed in 1611, although many small changes and improvements have been made in the text in subsequent editions. *Authorized version.* It was undertaken in the reign of James I. upon the recommendation of Dr. Reynolds, an influential clergyman and bishop of Norwich, of Puritan sympathies. *Executed by forty-seven learned men.* By the king's command forty-seven learned men entered upon the execution of the work. They were divided into six companies, two of which sat at Westminster, two at Oxford, and two at Cambridge. All previous editions, with all available manuscripts of original versions, were before them. They followed as closely as the authorities they consulted would admit, by command, the edition then in use, and called the "Bishop's Bible," because Archbishop Parker had supervised its preparation.

[50] Kitto's Biblical Cyclopedia. [51] The Canon of the New Testament, p. 429.

Of the result of their labors the editor of the "Annotated Paragraph Bible" remarks: "It would be too much to affirm that it is not susceptible of improvement; but its general excellence is attested by the fact, that with all the diversities of opinion on religious subjects, and the controversies which have been carried on between different denominations of Christians in our country, all have agreed in appealing to the same version, and none have, in any matters of consequence, objected to it."

Character of our version.

The revival of letters upon the introduction of the art of printing, especially the quickening influences of the Reformation and the influential example of Luther; the appeal from a professedly infallible Church to the inspired records of truth; the differences of doctrinal opinions in the Reformed Churches, all seeking their justification in the letter of Scripture; the searching examination given to the mythical fables, forming the beginning of all profane history; the extraordinary advances made in all the physical sciences, some of them apparently showing discrepancies and contradictions in the statements of the Bible; altogether turned with great zeal the thoughts and studies of scholars, both friendly and unfriendly, to the original sources of the records of a divine revelation. Impelled by the two strongest of human passions, hatred and love, the work has been going on until the present day. From ancient libraries, institutions of learning, rabbinical schools, and convents, gathered with the most persistent and patient labor, every scrap of manuscript containing the whole or portions of the various versions of the

Effect of the discovery of printing.

Examination of the original sources.

Bible, which we have already described, has been examined and collated; every site of the occurrence of scriptural incidents has been visited; human history has been reviewed; the hieroglyphics of Egypt and the sublime revelations of the earth's strata have been made to yield up their long-hidden secrets in these extended investigations. When this sifting and exhausting examination of the received Scriptures commenced many good men looked upon it with anxiety, fearing that the popular confidence in the genuineness and purity of the text might be destroyed. Their fears were unfounded. The Bible, like pure gold, only shone the brighter after the fiery trial. "A wonderful divine ordination," says Olshausen, "has preserved it to us without any essential injury through a succession of dark ages. It exerts at the present day upon all minds receptive of its spirit the same blessed, sanctifying influence which the apostles claimed for it eighteen centuries ago. How, then, can these sacred books suffer from careful historical inquiry respecting their origin? Investigation must rather serve to confirm and fully establish belief in their purity and genuineness."[52] When the learned Professor Bengel, of Tubingen, announced the forty thousand various readings which had been obtained from the different manuscript copies of the New Testament collated, it was feared at first that an entirely new version would be required; but it was found upon examination that the sense of the authorized edition was scarcely altered by them all; no previously held

marginal notes: The effect of this investigation feared at first. Those fears unfounded. Variations of Bengel.

---

[52] Olshausen's Commentaries, vol. I, p. 80.

or contested doctrine was affected in the slightest measure, and only one important passage, the well-known seventh verse of the fifth chapter of the First Epistle of John, relating to the three witnesses, was found to be sustained by so few original versions as to be marked unreliable. But the doctrine of the triune personality of God is not affected by the loss of this proof-text. Upon the result of these careful collations of original authorities Olshausen remarks: "Now that all the manuscripts have been read and accurately collated, there is no further occasion for fear that somewhere or other something new may be discovered which will thrust the old, loved Bible aside." [53] Some of these "various readings," considered of the most value, have been introduced into side columns in our reference Bibles, and sometimes, although rarely, they shed considerable light upon the text.

No doctrine affected.

No further fear.

Of the fifty thousand various readings which at the present time have been collected, the most of them are simply differences in orthography, punctuation, or a change in a particle, as *and* for *also;* and in the tenses, numbers, and cases of the words. Says Prof. Norton, in his work upon the genuineness of the Gospels: "It seems strange that the text of Shakspeare, which has been in existence less than two hundred and fifty years, should be far more uncertain and corrupt than that of the New Testament, now over eighteen centuries old, during nearly fifteen of which it existed only in manuscript. The industry of collators and commentators

The nature of these variations.

Prof. Norton upon the "various readings."

---

[53] Olshausen's Commentaries, vol. 1, p. 30.

indeed has collected a formidable array of 'various readings' in the Greek text of the Scriptures, but the number of those which have any good claim to be received, and which also seriously affect the sense, is so small that they may almost be counted upon the fingers. With perhaps a dozen or twenty exceptions, the text of every verse in the New Testament may be said to be so far settled by the general consent of scholars that any dispute as to its meaning must relate rather to the interpretation of the words than to any doubts respecting the words themselves. But in every one of Shakspeare's thirty-seven plays there are probably a hundred readings still in dispute, a large proportion of which materially affect the meaning of the passage in which they occur."

We may, then, answer the question with confidence, that we have in our English Bibles the revelation of God's will as it was given to the holy men that received it. Question answered.

CHAPTER IV.

INTERPRETATION: GENERAL OBSERVATIONS.

THE term *hermeneutics*, from the Greek word used by the apostle Paul, and translated the "*interpretation* of tongues,"[1] is the title used to designate the science or art of interpretation.

Hermeneutics.

The grand office of biblical interpretation is to discover the exact teaching of the Holy Spirit in the words uttered by inspired men. It is not its province to inquire how far any preconceived opinion finds justification in the Scriptures of truth, but simply and always "what the Spirit of Christ which was in them did signify."[2]

Office of biblical interpretation.

There are many peculiarities in the construction and character of the book which render its interpretation difficult, and require the closest and most careful study. Its first publication in the idioms of tongues foreign to our own—its constant allusion to customs unfamiliar to our days—its singular varieties of style, historical, poetical, prophetical—its sublime supernatural revelations of truth and spiritual life—all together make it a volume which study can never exhaust, and which it can never enter upon without the most enriching results.[3]

Peculiarities of book rendering its interpretation difficult.

---

[1] 1 Cor. xii, 10.   [2] 1 Peter i, 11.

[3] Dr. Stowe remarks in his inaugural address upon the "Interpretation of the Scriptures," when he entered upon his duties as a professor at Andover: "We

THE WORD OF GOD OPENED. 69

If one should ask why a book that contains truths so vital to our present and eternal well-being has not been given to man in a style so clear and simple that an ordinary mind could comprehend it upon the bare reading, and why it should be given to him as an

Why has God permitted it to be so difficult of comprehension?

have scarcely anything in common with them (the Jewish people) except a common humanity, and the same Deity; a common depravity, and the need of the same method of salvation; and it is precisely because we have these most important things in common with them that the Bible on these topics is so plain and intelligible to the humble, believing, prayerful inquirer. We have the same sun and moon and stars, and yet we can hardly be said to have the same heavens over our heads or the same earth beneath our feet, so different were their skies and fields and forests from ours. Instead of being like them in habits of life and modes of thought, our inner and outer life is as wholly unlike that of the ancient Hebrews as a modern cotton factory is unlike Solomon's temple, and the difference is very much of the same kind. In the application of science and art, for example, to the uses and conveniences of life they were infinitely behind us. In contrast with our numerous facilities for journeying and transportation, the Hebrews knew nothing of a *road* (1 Sam. xxvii, 10) as we understand the word road; they had no idea of any such thing as a bridge, and there is but one instance in the whole Hebrew history of so great a convenience as a ferry-boat, and that was in the latter part of the reign of their greatest king, and is alluded to as a luxury for the king's household, (2 Sam. xix, 18.) The distaff for spinning and the loom worked by hand were all the machinery they had for manufacturing cloth; of sugar and coffee and tea they had never heard; hair combs and pocket knives, and even pockets, were quite unknown to them; wheelbarrows and threshing machines, (their wheat was trodden out by oxen, or beaten out by sticks,) steam-engines and carding machines and nail factories they had never formed an idea of; paper and quills, steel pens and wafers, they had never used; and instead of our stereotype plates and power presses, striking off a whole Bible in two minutes, they had no way of making books but by a process which for facility and speed of writing was very much like engraving on copperplate, or cutting letters on a tombstone. Their very language and their mode of using language was in almost everything the reverse of ours. Their primitive words are verbs instead of nouns; they gave names to actions before they gave names to things; their books begin where ours end, and when we read their writings we always seem to ourselves to be reading backward. They wrote consonants only, and had no use for vowels. What we express

unexplored mine, with its hidden veins of gold and silver, long eluding the sight of the seeker after truth? the answer need not be, reverently, "Even so, Father, for so it seemed good in thy sight," alone; but other reasons at once suggest themselves to the thoughtful mind. The Bible was intended to be a study for man for all time. It reveals God. Every new discovery of the meaning and force of revelation is a fresh revelation of some aspect of the divine character. The necessity of constant study holds every generation in close connection with the divine mind, and becomes the medium through which God constantly communes with our race.

<small>Intended to be a study for all ages.</small>

A wonderful analogy we notice here between the revelations of God in the natural world and in his Scriptures. God has made all life a discipline. All our personal wants can only be supplied by labor and care and thought, and even faith, a process which, although it is wearisome, is wholesome, for it is the great school in which God develops and trains human minds. What is indispensable to life lies near to us; but its comforts and luxuries are to be sought for as hidden treasures. Every year man is discovering by study some new element in the divine economy which will add to his enjoyment. How many years the world lived without a knowl-

<small>Analogy with human life.</small>

<small>What is vital is near to us. Luxuries concealed.</small>

---

directly by a simple noun, they often designate by a picture; as for example, the pupil of the eye, because it always reflects a little image of the person looking into it, they call it *the little man, the eye's daughter*. They loved to give utterance to their thoughts in symbols and in types, in allegories and parables and riddles, and all their literature abounds with expedients of this kind."—*Bibliotheca Sacra*, 1853, p. 45.

edge of the hidden powers of electricity and steam, and how long men have walked over mines of gold and silver, and near mountains of coal and rivers of oil, and sailed over the most precious pearls! And the world is not yet exhausted, neither will it be until it is refined in its final fires.[4] Thus is it with the Scriptures. Sufficient relating to the salvation of the soul to lead a penitent man to forgiveness and to the door of heaven can be found in all parts of Scripture, and he that runneth may read. If every portion of the Bible should be lost but the fifteenth chapter of St. Luke, and the third chapter of St. John, we should still have the whole plan of salvation—the love of God, the atonement of Christ, the repenting sinner, and the changed heart, but beyond this there are still undiscovered continents of truth, facilities for the sanctification of human life, treasures of unutterable price hidden away in the stores of revelation, not to mock the earnest seeker, but to reward his zeal and add to his spiritual wealth. The prayer offered a thousand years ago still lingers upon devout

This is true of the Scriptures.

Prayer of David.

[4] Says the author of Ecce Deus, "God's first book, the book of nature, apparently leaves much of life unprovided for; yet as men acquire skill to turn over the ponderous pages they find that every want has been anticipated. Adam would hardly know the world of which he was the first occupant, yet the primal forces and characteristics of nature are just the same as when he kept the garden of Eden. Modern civilization can hardly understand how men could subsist in ancient times, yet the earth abideth forever without appendix or supplement. What was wanting was the faculty of interpretation. Men saw the water, but could not interpret it into steam; they saw the lightning, but mistook it for an enemy; they saw the sun, but could not fully interpret all he signified by the eloquence of light. The human power of interpretation grows, yet after it has grown it often forgets both the process and the fact. The volume of nature is precisely to-day as God published it, but the latter readers are more sharp-sighted and inquisitive than the former."—Page 24.

lips: "Open thou mine eyes, that I may behold wondrous things out of thy law."[5]

Dr. Schaff, remarking upon the New Testament and its language, says that the latter is the Macedonian Greek as spoken by the Jews of the dispersion in the time of Christ, and adds: "The most beautiful language of heathendom and the venerable language of the Jews are here combined, baptized with the spirit of Christianity, and made the picture of silver for the golden apple of the eternal truth of the Gospel. And, indeed, the style of the Bible in general is singularly adapted to men of every class and grade of culture, affording the child the simple nourishment for its religious wants, and the profoundest thinker inexhaustible matter of study. The Bible is not simply a popular book, but a book of all nations, and for all societies, classes, and conditions of men."[6]

<small>Dr. Schaff on language and character of the Bible.</small>

Locke has well said: "Men have reason to be well satisfied with what God has done for them, since he has given whatever is necessary for convenience of life and information of virtue, and has put within their reach, if they are willing to make search—to which, however, he will not compel them—a comfortable provision for this life, and the way that leads to a better. We shall not have much need to complain of the narrowness of our minds if we will employ them about what may be of use to us; and it will be an unpardonable as well as childish peevishness if we undervalue the advantages of our knowledge, and neglect to improve it because there are some things that are set out of its reach."

<small>Locke upon this feature of divine economy.</small>

[5] Psalm cxix, 18. [6] History of the Christian Church, vol. i, p. 93.

"Has not the natural world," says Goulburn,[1] "wondrous things, many and inexhaustible—wonders on a large scale, and wonders on a small? First, it has beautiful landscapes, which it asks no effort to admire, which we have only to open our eyes and behold. And, though landscapes vary in beauty, there are perhaps fewer than we imagine in which a contemplative eye can discover nothing of the beautiful. As it is with Scripture, so it is with nature; familiarity with it has a tendency to blunt our perceptions of its beauty. It does not follow from hence that the portions of nature which lie in our immediate vicinity contain no wonders. Wonders there may be in abundance, but they only reveal themselves to those who are at the pains of investigating them. As the rich man lazily rolls along in his carriage, and indolently complains of the tameness of the landscape, there may be wondrous things in the geological strata beneath his feet: fossil animals; evidences of volcanic agency. There may be gold dust in the streams; nay, as at Cracow, it may happen that in the earth's bowels there shall be lofty vaulted palaces of rock-salt, which appear by the light of flambeaux like so many crystals, or precious stones of various colors, casting a luster which the eye can scarcely bear. A slight amount of research and exertion would reach and discover these things, and would turn a residence in an otherwise tame country into a perpetual feast of curiosity. Then there are the wonders to which the telescope opens our eyes. It reveals to us worlds lit up by a common lamp

Nature as apparent to the eye.

Wonders hidden under our feet.

Wonders of the telescope.

[1] Devotional Study of the Scriptures, page 47.

with our own, several of them larger than our earth; and numbers of flaming balls scattered in brilliant profusion over the midnight sky, which, perchance, serve as suns of other systems. The astronomer will patiently watch for hours, exposed to the night-dews and the cold, to ascertain the truth in regard to some phenomenon of the heavens. There are the no less marvelous wonders of the microscope. By this is revealed to us a plurality of worlds in the most contracted limits, as the telescope had revealed to us a plurality in the vast reaches of space. All this admits of a close application to the Scriptures. The only difference is that the wondrous things of God's law are greater and more marvelous by far than anything which meets us in his works, for we are told that he has magnified his word above all his name, that is, above everything connected with him. Scripture has its more interesting and less interesting districts as they appear *upon the surface*. It has its sublime chapters upon the creation, its unequaled psalms, and its soul-moving parables. It has, also, its less imposing surfaces, its flats and levels, its *apparent* wastes. It has its long genealogical chapters, with no biographical sketches to enlighten them. It has its protracted ceremonial details, and it has its tangled brushwood and wild jungles in the perplexities which some of the prophetical writings seem to present, and which perhaps are never designed to be wholly cleared. It does not follow that these less interesting passages contain nothing beneath the surface worthy of research, and which will abundantly repay investigation. The richest mines have been found beneath the

Wonders of the microscope.

These illustrations apply to Scripture.

Rich mines beneath the surface.

most sterile and desolate tracts of earth. Every part of Scripture contains some lesson that subserves a useful purpose in the system of divine grace. They may lie hidden very deeply with the design of exciting curiosity and research. 'It is the glory of God to conceal a thing; but the honor of kings is to search out a matter.'"

Who does not see at once that this great variety, and often difficulty, and sometimes mystery, add to the attractiveness of Scripture, and occasion the necessity for that study and thought, without which its truths would avail us but little? An ordinary author is soon exhausted, and loses his power over us; but the Bible never, if thoughtfully read.* Without mental exertion a man may

Add to attractiveness of Scripture.

---

* Abundant testimony of the power of the Scriptures to reward with the highest form of intellectual and spiritual enjoyment their careful and protracted study might be given. At a late Bible anniversary Rev. Dr. Peabody, preacher and pastor at Harvard College, remarked: "I rejoice that we have a record of revelation that demands study, and a life-long study. It is one of the marks of the divine inspiration which fills this book, that its study demands, and crowns, and exceeds a life-time. If I had my life to live over again, I would be willing to devote the solid portion of my days to the study of St. Paul's Epistles. I should feel that in these alone there is work enough and joy enough for a life-long scholarship." And he adds, "Let it not be forgotten, that as the sweetest pastures are found among the rocks, so among those crags and cliffs in which is the hiding of the divine wisdom, among the least intelligible portions of the divine word, are found scattered those sweet and precious sentences on which the devout feed, and which have been the greatest of boons to generation after generation of the saints. One of the surest tokens to my mind of the divine inspiration of this book is the fact that strewn all over it are those passages of concentrated, condensed power, in which the sacred writers put into half a dozen words what would be weakly expressed in half a dozen pages or chapters."

"Where is the uninspired book," writes the late venerable Dr. William Marsh, "of which one can say, 'I never tire of reading it?' There is a book which I think I must have read fifty times, and I have not done with it yet. In a sense, I doubt whether I shall have done with it in *time*, for it is in *eter*

admire Scripture, even as without bodily exertion he may admire nature. If, however, he would profit by nature's resources, he must exert himself, digging the well, felling the timber, building the house, sinking the mine; so he must operate upon the crude material of Scripture, and look into its secret recesses with the energy and perseverance that he puts forth to meet his bodily wants. In the Old Testament we read what seems to be only a merciful provision for a patient burden-bearing beast: "Thou shalt not muz-

Man must exert himself to be able to use the resources of nature.

Illustration of truth hidden in Scripture.

nity we shall know fully its wondrous contents." The eminent Dr. Constantine Tischendorf, still blessing the Church with his untiring labors, has employed all his erudition, and all his time for more than twenty years, upon the textual study of the New Testament. When he discovered, after extraordinary endurance and perseverance, the ancient manuscript of the New Testament, some one thousand five hundred years old, in the convent of Mount Sinai, he hurried to his chamber, that, as he said, "he might give way to the transports of joy which he felt." "I knew that I held in my hand," he adds, "the most precious biblical treasure in existence; a document whose age and importance exceeded that of all the manuscripts which I had ever examined during *twenty years' study* of the subject. I cannot now, I confess, recall all the emotions which I felt in that exciting moment with such a diamond in my possession. Though my lamp was dim, and the night cold, I sat down at once to transcribe the 'Epistle of Barnabas,'" which was bound up with this edition of the New Testament, and of invaluable service in the argument demonstrating the genuineness and authenticity of our present New Testament canon. Honors from crowned heads and ancient universities, and even from Pius IX. himself, fell thickly upon him when his great work of publishing a fac-simile of the manuscripts was completed. But he mentions with undisguised pride his greater satisfaction with the remark of an old man, "himself of the highest distinction for learning:" "I would rather have discovered this Sinaitic manuscript than the koh-i-noor of the queen of England." How noble his remark: "That which I think more highly of than all these flattering distinctions is the conviction that Providence has given to our age, in which attacks on Christianity are so common, the Sinaitic Bible, to be to us a full and clear light as to what is the word written by God, and to assist us in defending the truth by establishing its authentic form."

zle the ox when he treadeth out the corn."⁹ This truth it certainly teaches, but within its folds we are taught by an inspired apostle is wrapped up an eternal principle of equity — that "the laborer is worthy of his reward."¹⁰

The Bible constantly presents general principles, absolute commandments, and living examples; but it never applies these principles to human actions as recorded upon its pages. This is left to the enlightened conscience and thoughtful judgment of the reader. It is His will that we should meditate upon all Scripture, and make ourselves their moral application. *Man must apply principles.* The Bible records the pious obedience and simple and singular faith of Noah, but makes no comment upon it; and it relates the story of his shame when overcome by his appetite, without a note of warning. *Illustration of fact and character without application of moral.* Abraham is sometimes called the friend of God, and is styled in Scripture the "father of them that believe." His marvelous simplicity of character and unfaltering trust in God are fully described in the sacred word, and, without note or comment or excuse, the stories of his deceit are also written out. God's abhorrence of Jacob's falsehood is not stated in the sacred narrative, neither his judgment as to a plurality of wives, it is left to be gathered from the after-fortunes of the patriarch, the retributions that fell upon him in his fears of Esau, and in his overwhelming domestic troubles. It was only in his later years that his life was gilded with gleams of comfort."¹¹ David is said, without reservation, to be a "man after God's

---

⁹ Deuteronomy xxv, 4.   ¹⁰ 1 Timothy v, 18.   ¹¹ Goulburn.

own heart;"[12] but what frightful sins the hand of inspiration, without hesitation, records against him. God leaves the strange extremes of his life for us to reconcile. Not one word of apology does he offer. David in Scripture is not presented as a saint, not even when judged by the defective standard of the times in which he lived. As compared with Saul, who refused to carry out God's commands, he was a chosen, faithful, and successful instrument; in this respect simply he was after God's heart. His sins were shocking, and the temporal retribution that followed fearful. His humility, his penitence, and his trust were as marvelous as his human weaknesses. In recording the end of Judas, where a human writer could hardly have failed to remark upon the added guilt of suicide and the steps which led to it, the reader is left to draw his own lessons as to the awful risk of sinning against high privileges, and constantly violating the convictions of conscience.

David and his sins.

Judas.

All these lessons require thought and study to elicit.

The distinction between simple attention to the literal word of inspiration and careful thought and study upon the truth which the Holy Spirit seeks to teach us by it has been happily illustrated by Dr. Goulburn. Attention to any book or discourse is that which serves, and which is necessary to enable us to retain the various points it sets forth in our memory. For example, we read the beautiful narrative of the Syrophœnician mother's appeal to our Lord in behalf of her daughter. Attention,

Distinction between attention and thought illustrated.

[12] 1 Sam. xiii. 14.

exercised while that story is read, will enable us to answer the following questions: Where was our Lord when this event happened? (It is said he was in the coasts of Tyre and Sidon.) Of what plague did the woman entreat our Lord to make her daughter whole? (It is said she was grievously vexed with a devil.) How did he at first receive her petition? (He answered her not a word.) How did the disciples beg him to act? (They besought him, saying, Send her away, for she crieth after us.) Suppose some one has read the narrative, or has heard it read in such a manner that, being afterward asked the above questions, he has been able to answer them all correctly, that person has exercised attention, and this is well; but it is not a profiting by the Scriptures; it is only an essential process *preliminary to the profiting by them.* The knowledge of the points of the story, which is secured by attention, is precisely the sort of knowledge with which we aim at filling the minds of children in our Sunday-schools. And it is to be feared that we are too apt to plume ourselves on the large stock of this sort of knowledge which a child of average intelligence will in a short time acquire. We forget that except as an essential preliminary to a far deeper and more important process, the knowledge of scriptural facts is absolutely worth nothing.

<small>Failure in Sunday-school instruction.</small>

Let us now consider what thought is, as distinct from attention.

A lower form of thought, which might operate upon the difficulties of the narrative, might awaken a speculative interest. Thus it might occur to one's mind that at this period our Lord is represented as being *out of the limits of Palestine*, (in the coasts of Tyre and Sidon,) and that at the same time there were other scriptural considerations leading us to believe that he never was out of those limits, the Lord being a minister to the circumcision, and sent only to the "lost sheep of the house of Israel;" we might seek the solution of the difficulty by inquiring whether the words might not be interpreted as meaning only the *borders* of Tyre and Sidon, (a district immediately adjoining this Gentile country.) This would be a form of speculative thought, which forms largely the field of inquiry among *critical* commentaries.

Speculative thought.

But there is a higher form of thought requisite to secure our obtaining from the Holy Scriptures that nourishment which we need. It brings into exercise not the speculative faculty, nor curiosity in any form or shape, but those moral faculties which the humblest mind has in common with the philosopher—the heart, the conscience, and the will. Devotional or practical thought will ask, Why did our Lord, so full of tenderness and compassion, who seems to have traveled into this far corner of Palestine for the sole purpose of giving this woman an opportunity of access to him, meet her with perfect silence, in the first instance, and in the second with the discouragement of rough, hard words? Why? but because he designs to teach me that if he does not immediately answer my prayers on the first application it is not that he does not hear them; it is to draw me on by apparent denial to greater earnestness and importunity in prayer, and to impress upon my heart

Devotional thought.

this lesson of lessons, that even if after earnest prayer things seem to go wrong, and my wishes seem to be thwarted, he has still a heart of love toward me beneath this disguise of stern severity.

> "Judge not the Lord by feeble sense,
> But trust him for his grace;
> Behind a frowning providence
> He hides a smiling face."

I understand now the meaning of the severe cross which I sometimes meet when I have earnestly devoted myself to God's service. Providence seemed to be thwarting me and discouraging me when engaged in prosecuting my religious duties; but this Scripture, as the voice of the Master, speaks to me and says, "Persevere; pray oftener and more earnestly; never abandon the narrow path of duty, however many discouragements are in it, and it shall be unto thee according to thy faith." And so, through the patience and comfort of the Scriptures, I have hope. *Meaning of discouragements.*

Thus we see how devotional thought discovers in the revealed word the very marrow of the Gospel, and makes it to be the food and comfort of the soul. *Devotional thought finds the marrow of the Gospel.*

I. It is of importance that the Bible should be studied in order to be properly interpreted as a whole or a unit. It contains but one revelation, and like a perfect body, every member has some vital relation to the whole frame. Christ is revealed in it from the commencement to the close. He comes first in promise, then in the ceremonial law, always in providential history, now in the *The whole Bible to be studied.*

strains of holy hymns, now in the glowing numbers of prophecy, at the appointed time is made manifest in the flesh, and is then held forth to the close of the canon as the expected triumphant King coming in the clouds of heaven.[13] The custom of spending so long a period

Christ in the whole Bible.

---

[13] As an illustration of the manner in which the whole revelation may be made to pour its light upon one truth, we append the response of two teachers at a late normal convention to the question as to the manner of showing the connection between the Passover and Christ's great sacrifice for sin: " *C.* I think I should call the attention of the class first to Genesis iv, 3–5, ' And Cain brought of the fruit of the ground an offering unto the Lord. And Abel, he also brought of the firstlings of his flock and of the fat thereof. And the Lord had respect unto Abel and to his offering : but unto Cain and to his offering he had not respect.' And I should tell my class that here was proof that a Lamb of God was chosen from the foundation of the world, since here a lamb is revealed as the only acceptable offering for sin ; and that this lamb was a type of Christ. I should then ask them to turn to Genesis xxii, 7, where we find in Abraham's offering of his son Isaac the wonderful connection between the lamb and a human body, foreshadowing again, with almost the distinctness of the very substance itself, the offering of Jesus. And when Abraham answers to Isaac's question, ' My son, God will provide himself a lamb,' I should ask, ' O, I wonder if Abraham knew the full meaning of his own reply, and whether he believed that God would provide for himself a lamb, or provide himself for a lamb ?' Then again in Exodus xxiii, 18, God calls this paschal lamb ' my sacrifice '—the sacrifice chosen of God, and God chosen for a sacrifice. Then I should refer them to John i, 29, in connection with Genesis xxii. 7, ' My son, God will provide himself a lamb,' and ' Behold the Lamb of God !' In his first epistle, i, 19. Peter says, ' A Lamb without blemish and without spot ;' John says, ' the Lamb of God ;' and in Isaiah liii, 7 the evangelical prophet says of Jesus, ' He was brought as a lamb to the slaughter.' In Exodus xii, 46 we read of the lamb that was prepared for the Passover. ' Neither shall ye break a bone thereof ;' and in John xix, 33, 36, ' And when they came to Jesus they brake not his legs, that the Scripture might be fulfilled, A bone of him shall not be broken.' And in Rev. v, 12 we read of ten thousand times ten thousand of the redeemed singing, ' Worthy is the Lamb that was slain ;' and once more, in Revelation xv, 3, that ' they sing the song of Moses the servant of God and the song of the Lamb.' "

" *Supt.* We shall only have time now to ask Brother P. what practical application he would make of this lesson to his scholars."

" *P.* I think I should tell my class that the slaying of the lamb and the

in Sunday-schools upon the study of local portions of Scripture to the neglect of others, and of the study of the Bible as a whole, destroys in the minds of the young the vital idea of the harmony of its parts, and depreciates the value of those portions of the holy record not ordinarily submitted to the study of a class. Why should years be spent upon the story of Christ in the Gospels when he is to be found in every portion of Holy Scripture?

In the same connection it should be remembered that there is a striking progress in revelation from its dawn to the last vision in the Apocalypse. It is a progress in nearly every respect in the development of God's spiritual kingdom upon the earth, as to the comprehension of it by those to whom it is revealed, and as to its requirements in order to secure the divine mercy. This thought

Revelation progressive.

sprinkling of the blood in the way of God's appointment was the means God had provided to bring the Israelites out of their cruel bondage. I would endeavor to show my scholars that they have sinned, and in common with the whole race, are under the bondage of sin. a bondage more cruel and relentless than that of the Israelites. and that God has provided a way of deliverance from this bondage; that Christ is that way; that his shed blood is the only means that God will use; and that this blood must be applied to the heart if the destroying angel, the avenging justice of God, shall pass over that heart. I should try to show that it matters not what the previous condition or character of the inmates of the house had been if only the blood was found sprinkled on the doorposts, and so it matters not how greatly we have sinned against God if Jesus's blood is sprinkled on the door of our hearts we are safe. Now how shall we apply this blood of Christ, and appropriate it to our own souls? Well, I should say that obedience to God's command on the part of the Israelites was an evidence of their faith; so, if we obey God's command to believe on the sacrifice he has appointed for sin. we exercise faith in the power and efficacy of his blood to save us. and faith therefore appropriates the sacrifice and saves us. And I might say at the close that each house had to have for itself the sign of blood upon it in order to salvation. so each soul must be sprinkled for itself with the blood of Christ or it will be eternally lost."

will aid the Bible student in comprehending many of the acts in human lives, as recorded in God's word, which did not, at the time they were committed, through the darkness of the dispensation, destroy the sensibility of conscience, or remove from them the favor of God. Dr. Chalmers, referring to the in-

Dr. Chalmers on a progressive standard of morality. cidents of deceit, inordinate indulgence, and even social crime in men that seemed really to enjoy communion with God, and some of them to be able to write spiritual hymns and prayers that penitent and pious men in all ages can adopt as the expression of their own emotions, remarks, that these examples, set forth in Scripture without reprobation, "are fitted to stagger those who reflect not sufficiently on the incapacity of our narrow faculties with their limited range to pronounce on all the objects and history of the divine administration. Though morality in the abstract is unchangeable, it looks as if in the concrete there was a *progressive morality* from one era to another, an accommodation to the ruder and earlier periods of humanity, distinctly intimated by our Saviour when he tells us of polygamy being allowed before the times of the Gospels, because of the hardness of their hearts. It is worthy of remark that there is no example, as far as I can recollect, of any deception or imperfect morality of any sort being recorded of Christian disciples in the New Testament without a prompt and decided condemnation, as in the case of Paul rebuking Peter for his ambidextrous policy between Jews and Gentiles." [14]

Bernard on progress in the New Testament A late writer, Bernard, in his Bampton Lectures, has shown most convincingly the gradual

[14] Scripture Readings, vol. l, p. 2".

development of doctrines in the New Testament, from the revelation of the kingdom of heaven, coming without observation into human hearts, to the universal and triumphant kingdom over angels and men, as set forth in the book of Revelation; from the moral lessons of the sermon on the mount to the full development of the life of faith in the epistles of St. Paul; and from the penitent prodigal returning to the father's house to the moral Jewish counselor, pointed to the crucified Messiah as the means of securing the new birth through the agency of the Holy Ghost.[15] This view of the Bible makes *all* inspired Scripture "profitable for doctrine."

Olshausen remarks that "throughout Scripture there runs the doctrine of a deep, essential connection between the Old and New Testaments. As the Old Testament is always pointing onward to the New, so the latter is always pointing backward to the Old as its necessary precedent. Consequently, both alike bear the character of a divine revelation; only this revelation manifests itself in a gradual development. In the Old Testament it appears in its commencement as the seed of the subsequent plant; in the New Testament the living plant itself is exhibited. On account of this relation there cannot be any thing in the Old Testament specifically different from what is to be found in the New Testament, only the form of presenting the same thing is at one time more or less plain and direct than at another." [16]

Olshausen on unity and progress in Scripture.

[15] Progress of Doctrine in the New Testament, by Thomas D. Bernard, M.A.
[16] Commentaries, vol. i, p. 131.

II. In this connection it may be remarked that it is important to understand the scope of each book of the Bible, the especial revelation it proposes to make, the main object for which it was written, or the circumstances that called it forth. The best commentary upon some of the epistles is a knowledge of the occasion of their being written, and a careful reading of them through, instead of piecemeal by chapters, as they have been arbitrarily broken up for the benefit of reference.

The scope of each book to be understood.

Mr. Locke thus recommends the perusal of a book at a sitting. Referring to his own experience, he says: "I concluded that it was necessary, for the understanding of any one of them, (St. Paul's epistles,) often to read it all through at one sitting, and to observe, as well as I could, the design of his writing it. If the first reading gave me some light, the second gave me more; and so I persisted on, reading constantly the whole epistle over at once, till I came to have a good general view of the apostle's main purpose in writing."

Locke's habit of reading a book at a sitting.

Sometimes the sacred writer states with more or less definiteness his purpose, and his argument is to be read in view of this plan. An instance is found in Paul's Epistle to the Romans. In the first three chapters he thoroughly reviews the moral condition of Jews and Gentiles in all ages, and proves that the whole world is guilty before God. In the twentieth verse of the third chapter he states his main purpose is to show that "by the deeds of the law shall no flesh be justified in his sight; for by the law is the knowledge of sin." Having

Sometimes object of sacred writer stated by himself.

gained this, he proposes to answer the momentous question: "How *shall* a man be just with God?" After a clear and powerful discussion of the subject through the seven verses that follow, in the twenty-eighth he announces the evident result of his reasoning: "Therefore, we conclude that a man is justified by faith without the deeds of the law." This conclusion the apostle then proceeds to set forth and illustrate in its various relations to human experience and to God's previous dealings with his people.

The best commentators are not those that are the most profuse in notes upon separate words, but who give the general scope and meaning of the sacred writers. As you ruin a flower by tearing it in pieces, so our multiplied lessons upon limited portions of Scripture tear the divine record into tatters, destroy both its refreshing fragrance and its beauty, and really sacrifice its life and power."

The beauty and power of Scripture destroyed by considering it out of its connections.

[17] The interest that has been awakened in the ministry and among the people in the exposition of the Scriptures from the pulpit is a wholesome sign of the times. The Bible text is too often announced at the commencement of a sermon simply as a motto or a sentiment to distinguish the discourse from an ordinary lecture. There is no instrument placed by the Holy Spirit in the hands of a godly minister so powerful to save and to edify the Church as the Scriptures of truth. One of the ablest and most popular ministers of New York has crowded his church on Sabbath afternoons now for more than a year with expositions of the word of God in order, commencing with Genesis. No course can more effectually fortify the youth of the Church against the specious attacks upon the inspiration of the Bible now filling the literature of the age. Dr. M'Lelland somewhat tartly remarks: "Nor can we approve the practice adopted by many preachers, of running into their pulpits with a single sentence or part of one, which they make their exclusive subject, not bestowing on the connection a word of notice, unless they have been hurried in their preparations, and find it convenient to talk a little *round* it in an extempore intro-

Lessons upon the Gospels chronologically arranged have their purpose, but they divert the mind of the learner from a comprehension of the specific and important, because divine, character and object of each evangelist. Matthew presents the kingly side of our Lord's character, Mark the human, Luke the sacrificial, and John the divine.[18]

Each Gospel has a character of its own.

duction. What would we think if we heard any other book prelected on in this way—a treatise on medicine, for instance, or on morals? or, What would we think of a judge expounding in this way a legal statute? The civil law has laid down an express canon on the subject, as if indignant at the idea of such a practice. It says, (as translated :) ' Base is he to judge concerning the law, not having examined the entire law.' Ministers are often heard to chide their people sharply for the careless and unprofitable way in which they read the word of God ; but they would do well to ask whether they are not themselves to blame in forming them to such wretched habits of perusing it. When his reverence appears before the people month after month without, in a single instance perhaps, explaining the design, coherence, and argument of a paragraph containing only six verses, it is really too much to expect that honest John will spend his Sabbath evenings in supplying the pastor's lack of service."

[18] Bernard, in his Bampton Lectures upon the " Progress of Doctrine in the New Testament," thus happily presents the scope of revelation in the New Testament : " First, a person is manifested and facts are set forth in the simplest external aspect, under the clearest light, and with the concurrence of a fourfold witness. This witness also is itself progressive, and in the last Gospel the glory of the person has grown more bright, and the meaning of the facts more clear. Then in the book of Acts Christ is preached as perfected, and as the refuge and life of the world. The results of his appearing are summed up and settled, and men are called to believe and be saved. Those who do so find themselves in new relations to each other, they become one body, and grow into the form and life of a catholic (or universal) Church. The state which has thus been entered needs to be expounded, and the life which has been begun needs to be educated. The apostolic letters perform the work. The questions which universally follow the first submissions of the mind receive their answers, and so the faith which was general grows definite. The rising exigencies of the new life are met, both for the man and for the Church ; and we learn what is the happy consciousness, and what the holy conversation, which belong

III. In interpreting Scripture we are never to forget its character. It is not intended to be a revelation of science or a model of history, or to be judged simply as to the literature of its poetry. It proposes simply to reveal God's truth to all ages of men. *Scripture not a revelation of science.*

Dr. Stowe, in his interesting work upon the books of the Bible, remarks in a characteristically strong and perhaps somewhat extravagant way, "The Bible does not state, and never professes to state, scientific facts in scientific forms, but only phenomena or appearances to the eye of a spectator. For example, that the earth revolves on its axis from west to east once in twenty-four hours, thus producing day and night, is a scientific fact; this the Bible never states, nor even alludes to. Indeed, I do not suppose that the writers of the Bible knew anything about it, for 'inspiration is not omniscience.' That the sun rises in the east and passes along in the heavens till he sets in the west is a phenomenon, an appearance to the human eye, and this, and this only, is what the Bible speaks of, just as in the language *Dr. Stowe on unscientific character of Bible.*

to those who are *in* Christ Jesus. Lastly, as members of the body of Christ, we find ourselves partakers in a corporate life and a history larger than our own. We feel that we are taken up into a scheme of things which is in conflict with the present, and which cannot realize itself here. Therefore, our final teaching is by prophecy, which shows us, not how we are personally saved and victorious, but how the battle goes upon the whole, and which issues in the appearance of a holy city, in which redemption reaches its end, and the Redeemer finds his joy; in which human tendencies are realized, and divine promises fulfilled; in which the ideal has become the actual, and man is perfected in the presence and glory of God. . . . Only the written word of God, confidingly followed in the progressive steps of its advance, can lead the weakest or the wisest into the deep blessedness of the life that is in Christ, and into the final glory of the city of God."

of common life and common sense every-where, both among the learned and unlearned. While the statements of the Bible are true to the phenomena, the appearances, they are right; they have nothing to do with scientific facts, and cannot come into collision with them any more than the decisions of a judge in the supreme court can come in collision with the governor's coach, for the two subjects are not of the same kind, they belong to two entirely different spheres of thought; they do not travel at all in the same road, and how can they come in collision? To interpret the first chapter of Genesis as a geological essay, and to attempt to remove from it, by scientific methods, geological difficulties, seems to me like interpreting the parable of the sower as an agricultural essay, and attempting to avoid the difficulty that the fowls of the air devoured only the seed that fell by the way side, by learned inquiries as to whether birds in ancient times could fly over fences, and whether they were not obliged to keep the road, and solemnly imagining the sustaining of the latter supposition to be essential to the vindication of the truthfulness of Christ as a religious teacher. How much better to look at the simple fact just as it existed, to wit, that in the Eastern countries, as now in Germany and France, the farms were seldom fenced, and the fields for the most part were guarded by old men, women, and children, whose duty it was to keep away the birds as well as the cattle; and this practice very generally obtains in those countries at the present day, simply because that there old men, women, and children are cheaper than fencing stuff. In the interpretation of so plain and

Folly of interpreting the first of Genesis as a treatise upon geology.

THE WORD OF GOD OPENED. 9a

homely a book as the Bible a knowledge of the facts and good common sense are generally much better guides than scientific ingenuity or metaphysical subtilty. *Common sense an interpreter of the Bible.* The Bible was not written with reference to science or philosophy, but with reference to the feelings, impressions, and needs of the great masses of mankind, and they are neither scientific men nor philosophers."[19]

No Christian student need have anxiety lest any revelation in the natural world will ever contradict the Bible. Whatever discoveries are made in chronology as to the duration of man's previous residence upon earth, as to the origin of species, or in the hidden strata of the earth, *True science cannot harm the Bible.* the Christian scholar may patiently await their full development. They may be thrust forward in the interest of unbelief; but it will ever be in the future as in the past, that the revelations of all the sciences as they come to be fully understood will entirely accord with the tenor and spirit of God's word. The Bible is no nearer being an obsolete book than it was when the earth was supposed to be the center of the universe, and the whole celestial system was thought to have been created in exactly six days.

IV. The fact must not be overlooked that the Holy Scriptures are unsystematic. They contain no "body of divinity," and no connected catechism, with questions and answers. The attributes of God are gathered as they are disclosed in his providential government over his *The Bible unscientific.* people, or in various revelations through different inspired men, and in different forms. The doctrines of the Gospel

---

[19] Origin and History of the Books of the Bible, page 29.

relating to sin and human salvation are presented without order all over the sacred pages. One view will be presented at one time—as the love of God and the welcome with which he receives the penitent—and the indispensableness of the new birth at another. At one time Paul sets forth the vital character of faith, without which it is impossible to please God, and the helplessness of one who hopes to save himself simply by good works: while James, in view of a condition of things then existing in the Church, sets forth with great prominence good works as the only reliable human test of a correct faith. There can be no contradiction. All the views of all the sacred writers are true, but they need to be understood in harmony with each other, and must be interpreted in the light of the circumstances under which they were written. Goulburn remarks, "The precept and the doctrine (in the Scriptures) are thrown out just as the occasion for them offers. The sacred writer does not stop to guard or counterbalance them; if they need this, the counterbalancing precept is to be found in another inspired writing, which originated on a wholly different occasion. Even so in the field of nature we do not find a noxious herb growing side by side with its antidote; but noxious herbs (only noxious in certain applications, having their uses and services in the general system) are found in one locality; in another district, whose features are different, springs up the medicinal plant. Man is left to discover and apply the counteracting power."

[Margin: Different truths taught at different times.]
[Margin: Goulburn's illustration of this.]
[Margin: Analogy in nature.]

Overlooking this truth the great reformer himself, Martin

Luther, who had fought in his own person for the doctrine of salvation by faith only, was disposed to throw out of the canon the Epistle of James as teaching a different Gospel, and therefore not one of the divine circle. Luther was right in his doctrine according to Paul, and so was James. There was, in truth, no collision between them; but the reformer was too impatient in the stress of his struggle with the Roman Church to give the apostle a careful examination. Into this error those fall who affirm a finite and human nature only to the Son of God, and quote the words of Jesus himself to prove it; who insist that repentance without faith in the atonement is all that is requisite to secure the favor of God, and quote the parable of the prodigal son; and those also who predicate the final salvation of all upon the revealed doctrine of the Fatherhood of God. Their views are certainly to be found in portions of the inspired word, but they are essentially modified without being in the least nullified by distinct revelations found in other portions of the Bible, and readily harmonized when one is willing to receive the whole counsel of God. These Scriptures present but different sides of the same truth.

<small>Error of Martin Luther.</small>

<small>Error of Rationalists and Universalists.</small>

V. Here we may remark that the interpreter should not consider himself responsible for what is said or taught in the Scriptures. This revelation of God requires no apology from him. His simple office is to discover what the Holy Spirit teaches. It is not for him to soften any threatening, to modify any doctrine, to "explain away" the apparent meaning of any text, but simply to

<small>Interpreter not responsible for what God says.</small>

declare the evident sense of what "is written." Says Dr. Doedes, professor of divinity in the University of Utrecht: "Let the New Testament teach what it teaches; and if men do not agree with it, let them have the courage to say so.

Dr Doedes on the irresponsibility of interpreter if he gives the exact text. If men do not agree with it, it is because they think that they know better. Well, be it so. But let the New Testament have its own views. The task of the interpreter is verily not of such a nature that when he does his duty he need ever make himself feel anxious while employed upon it. But he must needs become anxious if he hold himself responsible for what is written there. This, then, however, is a cross that he lays on his own shoulders; and, alas! a source of torture to the writings which he has to interpret."[20] "Be very careful," he says in another place, "lest you make the Scriptures say what you would like to find in them. What have people not extracted from the New Testament? that is, What have people not introduced into it?" We should not forget that it is the truth of God that saves, not our opinion of what that truth should be.

VI. The earliest interpreters of Scripture, in order more readily to reconcile difficulties, and to combat the views of certain errorists, held to a figurative, symbolical, double, threefold, fourfold, and manifold meaning of the words of the sacred record. Origen taught that the literal word was valueless, and that even the Scripture histories were allegorical; that the six days of creation signified the renovation of the soul, the *six days* intimating that it was a

---

[20] Hermeneutics of the New Testament, page 59.

THE WORD OF GOD OPENED. 95

progressive work. Israel in Egypt is the soul living in error, and the seven plagues are its purgations from various evil habits; the frogs denoting loquacity, the fleas carnal appetites, the boils pride and arrogance, etc. As man is composed of body, mind, and soul, he taught that there was a threefold sense, the literal, the moral, and the spiritual, in which the truth of inspiration was to be considered. Origen, reading that Abraham married Keturah in his old age, and learning that Keturah meant in Hebrew "sweet odor," and esteeming "sweet odor" to be a scriptural figure of the fragrance of righteousness of character, taught that the true meaning of this passage was, that in his old age Abraham became eminently holy. These views, with various modifications, influenced the interpretation of Scripture, until the morning of the Reformation put to flight the clouds and fogs that had settled down upon the word of God. But one Church, that of the New Jerusalem, or the Swedenborgian, at the present day gives countenance to such a rendering of the Scriptures. Such a view makes the Bible not the revelation, but the obscuration, of the will of God. There is a tendency among some teachers to seek far-fetched and fanciful interpretations, especially of the Old Testament; as when the six steps by which Solomon ascended to his throne are made to represent the six steps a sinner takes to reach pardon and eternal life: conviction, repentance, faith, regeneration, justification, and sanctification. Upon the "instrument of ten strings" with which the Psalmist would praise God, Chrysostom discourses upon the Ten Commandments.

The Reformation changed this.

made delightful and easy to keep by divine grace. On the text, "Whereof every one beareth twins," he asks, "What twins?" and answers, "*The law and the prophets*—the two commandments whereon hang all in the life of every believer!" The *bread* and *fish* and *egg* which the child asks of his father in the parable are thus explained by him: the bread is the soul, the fish is faith, which lives amid the billows of temptation, and the egg is hope, a pledge of something, but not the chicken itself! This is always reprehensible and dangerous. The custom of giving lessons upon the blackboard in Sunday-schools tends, although not necessarily, to this habit of allegorizing the Scriptures.[21]

[21] Dr. Wise, in the "Sunday-School Journal" for March, 1868, makes the following well-deserved and appropriate criticism upon a "blackboard exercise" prepared as a model for the "Sunday-School Times:"

"'How to Prepare a Blackboard Exercise for a Sunday-School Lesson.

1. *Learn the lesson thoroughly;* get the head, and especially the *heart*, full of it, by hard study and earnest prayer.

2. Select *the thought* you wish to use.

3. *Condense* that thought to the *smallest* and *sharpest* point possible.

4. Place that *point* upon the board.

5. Remember that the *thought* or *outline* on the board is but "*dry bones*," until clothed with "thoughts that breathe and words that burn" from a warm and earnest heart.

EXERCISE:
Open Windows Dangerous for Sleepers.*
Acts xx, 9-12.

The open windows.	Place of safety.	The open windows.	Place of safety.
Ball room.		Gambling Saloons.	
Theater.	In Christ only.	Impenitence.	In Christ only.
Drinking Saloons.		Etc., etc.	

* Those *sleep in open windows* who do not realize the dangers to which they are exposed. Call upon the school to name the open windows. E. H. Y.
Plymouth, Ill.

The principle of interpretation which now prevails throughout the Christian Church is sometimes called the historico-grammatical mode. It affirms

Historico-grammatical mode of interpretation.

"The five canons here laid down are certainly very excellent, provided the *second* be properly qualified. 'Select *the thought* you wish to use.' Very good. But then that thought should be one that is obviously in the passage, or logically deducible from it. It should be the leading thought. But E. H. Y. in his 'exercise' violates his own canon by putting a 'thought' on the board which is *not selected* from the lesson he proposes to illustrate, because it is not in it at all. Let us look at it a moment.

"The lesson is Acts xx, 9-12, which records Paul's farewell sermon at Troas, the sleep of Eutychus at the open window, the fall and death of the sleeper, with his restoration to life by the apostle.

"From this passage, which was evidently recorded for the purpose of preserving an account of the miracle, and not to censure Eutychus for a slumber which, if not unavoidable, was certainly excusable under the circumstances, we have for a selected point,

"'OPEN WINDOWS DANGEROUS FOR SLEEPERS.'"

"Now if the lesson contained this proposition, to select it would show a singular avoidance of a grand illustration of divine power for the sake of bringing out an unimportant physical fact. But the proposition itself is neither in the lesson, nor is it true in itself.

"All that the lesson teaches about open windows and sleepers is, that it is dangerous for persons *to sleep in* open windows. But E. H. Y. says, its thought is 'open windows dangerous for sleepers,' a statement which omits the important fact that the danger arises not from the open windows but from sleeping in them. This omission makes the statement false, for open windows are often healthful, instead of being dangerous, to sleepers.

"True, E. H. Y. in his note attempts to explain his meaning, but the need he felt for the insertion of a qualifying note ought to have shown him that his proposition was defective. The 'thought' on a blackboard should be so put as not to need qualification. If it does, one object of the blackboard, which is to impress some great truth on the mind through the eye, is defeated. Scholars carry away the point *as it is written*, not as it is qualified by the speaker.

"This defect in his main point vitiates the logic of his whole 'exercise.' Who can see any connection between an open window and a ball room, a theater, or a drinking saloon? The note says the point of analogy is 'that those who sleep in open windows do not realize the dangers to which they are exposed,' etc. But this statement confuses the mind by changing the subject of the prop-

that the simple grammatical meaning of the text in its connections, modified only by what is requisite to be known

osition. In the stated point '*open windows*' constitute the subject; in the note, *those who 'sleep* in open windows.'

"Indeed, the note makes a new statement of the selected thought. It is no longer 'open windows dangerous to sleepers,' but those who sleep in open windows 'do not realize the danger to which they are exposed,' which is certainly nearer the truth than the other. But its introduction tends to confuse the mind of the scholar.

"Again, the 'exercise' is defective because it leaves its 'point' *unproven*. It assumes the ball room, etc., to be 'open windows,' but as there is no obvious analogy between an open window and a ball room, the assertion must fall without weight on the scholar's mind.

"But E. H. Y. will say, perhaps, that his note was intended to define the last term in his proposition—*sleepers*. Very good. Let us apply his definition to his figurative open windows—the ball room for example. How will it stand? Why thus: The 'ball room' is 'dangerous for sleepers,' that is, for those '*who do not realize the dangers to which they are exposed*.' Does not this make the danger lie, not in the thing itself, but in the failure of the ball room visitor to realize the true character of the place? Let him realize this, and become a conscious and willful sinner, and the ball room ceases to be an open window. What nonsense! Yet we have no doubt that this exercise, given by a good chalker and talker in a school or institute, would be regarded as very fine. Its ingenuity would divert attention from its fallacy.

"Finally, the whole exercise is far-fetched. It is absurd to argue that because Eutychus fell out of a window a child should beware of going to a ball or a theter. There are plenty of texts which could be properly applied to dangerous amusements; but to go to poor, sleepy Eutychus for an argument is like going from New York to Philadelphia by way of Albany. The journey is possible, but it is needlessly long. That such an exercise should be given as a model in such an excellent paper as the "Times," by one who is evidently a man of mental vigor, is a justification of our late caution to keep the blackboard out of unskillful hands. The blackboard is an educational Janus. It may be friend or foe to real instruction; therefore we say again, Use it sparingly, use it skillfully, or let it alone.

"We have written this criticism not to discourage the proper use of the blackboard, but to guard against its abuse. As an example of false syntax is often a better illustration of a grammatical rule than a correct rule, so may this criticism be a better help to one who uses the blackboard than a really faultless exercise."

about the language in which it was uttered, the individuality and custom of speaking of the author, and the manners and customs of the times, is the sense in which the Holy Ghost reveals his truth through the words of Scripture.

The proper office of the commentary, Bible dictionary, and other helps is to correct the text if there is any error, to give the modern meaning of the word if the old is obsolete, to aid in reconciling the difficulties of Scripture, and to present such facts in relation to the times and customs and homes of the writers as will enable us better to apprehend their meaning. We wish to obtain from learned men the exact force of the expressions used by the inspired writers; the doctrines and precepts involved in them we can apprehend ourselves. *Office of commentaries, etc.*

CHAPTER V.

PRELIMINARY STUDIES.

I. THIS volume is written to meet the wants of those who are only familiar with their native tongue—the great body of our Bible interpreters to the children of the land. Our own language is enriched with the choicest translations from other tongues of works of criticism and with commentaries upon the Holy Scriptures. Dictionaries and exegetical notes are readily obtained, and at comparatively small expense, by our Sunday-school teachers. But to those that are still young, and can, although at considerable sacrifice, secure the time for the acquisition of ability to read with some ease the Hebrew and Greek text, we would unhesitatingly say, the pleasurable and profitable results will be an ample compensation for all the requisite toil. The finest linguist of New England mastered the numerous tongues which he read and spake while prosecuting the laborious business of a blacksmith. It is not necessary to become critical scholars in order, by a general knowledge of the grammar, idioms, and meaning of the words, to be enabled better to appreciate and weigh the published results of the life-long scholarship and devotion to the work of biblical interpretation now the possession of the Christian Church. It is said of the Puritan Bradford that he mastered the Latin

[Marginal notes: Study of the original languages. Persons need not necessarily be critical scholars. Bradford the Puritan.]

and Greek, and studied the Hebrew, because "he would see with his own eyes the ancient oracles of God in their native beauty."

II. In order to appreciate the meaning, the force, and the beauty of the sacred writings, it is necessary to be familiar with the geography of biblical countries, and of the former and present appearance of Scripture places. *Should be familiar with biblical geography.* Of the effect of such a knowledge to confirm our confidence in the Bible, and to throw light upon its inspired pages, even Renan, the French Rationalist, says: "My commission led me to reside on the frontiers of Galilee, and to traverse it frequently. I have traveled through the evangelical province in every direction. *Testimony of Renan.* I have visited Jerusalem, Hebron, and Samaria. Scarcely any locality important in the history of Jesus has escaped me. All this history, which at a distance seems floating in the clouds of an unreal world, thus assumed a body, a solidity, which astonished me. The striking accord of the texts and the places, the wonderful harmony of the evangelical ideal with the landscape which served as its setting, were to me as a revelation. I had before my eyes a ifth Gospel, torn, but still legible, and thenceforth, through he narratives of Matthew and Mark, instead of an abstract being, which one would say had never existed, I saw a wonderful human form live and move."[1]

[1] Life of Jesus, page 45. We find in an English Sunday-school periodical a homely but significant illustration of the power of a knowledge of Scripture localities to confirm our faith in the sacred record: "In a Yorkshire village I knew one Thomas Walsh. It was a favorite opinion of Walsh's that the Bible was all made up.' He could never believe it was written where it professed

No one can listen to the lecture of Dr. Hibbard (author of a valuable treatise upon the Psalms) upon the journeyings of the Israelites in the wilderness, illustrated by his large charts, without receiving a fresh and most

Hibbard and Vincent.

to be, and by the men said to have written it. Walsh owned a considerable part of a factory, and one year he set his heart on making a very large and fine piece of cloth. He took great pains with the carding, spinning, dyeing, weaving, and finishing of it. In the process of manufacture it was one day stretched out on the tenter-hooks to dry. It made a fine show, and he felt very proud of it. The next morning he arose early to work at it, when, to his amazement, it was gone! It had been stolen during the night. After weeks of anxiety and expense, a piece of cloth, answering the description, was stopped at Manchester, awaiting the owner and proof. Away to Manchester went Thomas as fast as the express train would carry him. There he found many rolls of cloth which had been stolen. They were very much alike. He selected one which he claimed as his. But how could he prove it? In doubt and perplexity he called on his neighbor Stetson. 'Friend Stetson, I have found a piece of cloth which I am sure is the one which was stolen from me. But how to prove it is the question. Can you tell me how?' 'You don't want it unless it is really yours?' 'Certainly not.' 'And you want proof that is simple, plain, and such as will satisfy yourself and everybody?' 'Precisely so.' 'Well, take Bible proof.' 'Bible proof! Pray, what is that?' 'Take your cloth to the tenter-hooks on which it was stretched, and if it is yours every hook will just come to the hole through which it passed before being taken down. There will be scores of such hooks, and if the hooks and holes just come together right, no other proof that the cloth is yours will be wanted.' 'True. Why didn't I think of this before?' Away he hastened, and, sure enough, every hook came to its little hole, and the cloth was proved to be his, and the thief was convicted, all on the evidence of the tenter-hooks. Some days after this, Thomas again hailed his friend. 'I say, Stetson, what did you mean by calling tenter-hooks proof, the other day, "Bible proof?"' I am sure if I had the good evidence for the Bible that I had for my cloth, I would never doubt it again.' 'You have the same, only better, for the Bible.' 'How so?' 'Put it on the tenter-hooks. Take the Bible and travel with it; go to the place where it was made. There you find the Red Sea, the Jordan, the Lake of Galilee, Mounts Lebanon, Hermon, Carmel, Tabor, and Gerizim; there you find the cities of Damascus, Hebron, Tyre, Sidon, and Jerusalem. Every mountain, every river, every sheet of water mentioned in the Bible is there, just in the place where it

interesting version of the portions of the Pentateuch devoted to a record of these wanderings; and the map drawings and explanations of Rev. J. H. Vincent at Sunday-school institutes have suggested to hundreds the invaluable service which a familiar knowledge of this science affords the interpreter of Scripture.

"It is a common remark of historians concerning the Christians of the Middle Ages that their devotion was astonishingly increased by a pilgrimage to the Holy Land. This might be expected. They had gone over the hallowed ground, and were able to form a distinct picture of it. They had walked the streets of the city which their divine Saviour had honored with his ministrations, and trod the very mount on which he had been lifted up between heaven and earth. The vivid idea of the localities passed, by an easy transition, to all the facts and doctrines connected with them, and the felt reality of Calvary diffused itself over the sufferings which a thousand years before had been endured there."[2] *Effect of visiting holy places.*

As an instance of the new life which may be given to an ancient event let us extract a few sentences from the diary of Dean Stanley, kept during his memorable tour with the

is located. Sinai, and the desert, and the Dead Sea are there; so that the best guide-book through the country is the Bible. It must have been written there on the spot, just as your cloth must have been made and stretched on your tenter-hooks. That land is the mold in which the Bible was cast, and when brought together we see that they fit together. You might just as well doubt that your cloth was fitted to your hooks.' 'Well, well, I confess I never thought of that. I'll think it over again. If you are right, why, then, I'm wrong, that's all.'—*Bible C. Magazine.*

[2] Canon and Interpretation of Scripture. By Prof. M'LELLAND, page 137.

Prince of Wales over Palestine. We should be glad, had we space, to introduce the entire account of the visit to the old Abrahamic city of Hebron. After leaving the mosque, covering, with strong evidences of probability, the cave of Machpelah, where reposes the dust of several of the patriarchs and their wives, they "rode over the hills south of Hebron to visit the probable scene of the romantic transaction, recorded in the book of Joshua and the book of Judges, between Caleb and his daughter Achsah.[3] A wide valley, unusually green, amid the barren hills of the 'south country,' suddenly breaks down into an almost precipitous and still greener ravine. On the south side of this ravine is a village called *Dura*, possibly the *Adorami* of the book of Chronicles;[4] on the north, at the summit of a steeper and more rugged ascent, is *Dewer Dan*, which recalls the name of *Debir*, the fortress which Othniel stormed on the condition of winning Achsah for his bride. 'Give me,' she said to her father, as she rode on her ass beside him, 'a field,' (a blessing, a rich field, such as that which lies spread in the green basin, which she and Caleb would first encounter in their ride from Hebron,) 'for thou hast given me a south land,' (these dry rocky hills which extend as far as the eye can reach, till they melt into the hazy platform of the desert,) 'give me also the *bubblings* of water, the upper and lower bubblings.' It is an expressive word, (translated in our version upper and nether springs,) which seems to be used for *tumbling, falling waves*, and is thus especially applicable to the rare sight of a clear rivulet that,

---

[3] Josh. xv. 16-19; Judges i. 11-15. [4] 2 Chron. xi. 9.

THE WORD OF GOD OPENED.　　　105

rising in the green meadow above mentioned, falls and flows continuously down to the bottom of the ravine, and by its upper and nether streams gives verdure to the whole. The identification is not perhaps absolutely certain, but the scene lends itself to the incident in every particular."[5]

The full effect of personal examination we may not be able to enjoy; but in such works as Dr. Robinson's, Dean Stanley's, Thomson's "The Land and the Book," and Ritter's Geography of Palestine, we are enabled to look upon sacred localities almost as distinctly as if we gazed upon them with our own eyes. *Works that give us a vivid idea of holy localities.* All fulfilled prophecy, both of the Old and New Testaments, relating to ancient countries and cities, finds the most impressive confirmation in the present appearance of these memorable lands. *Importance of this as to fulfilled prophecy.* There is continued reference in the Old Testament to a gigantic race beside whom the Jewish spies were as grasshoppers.[6] They were the original inhabitants of Bashan, east of the Jordan, and probably of Canaan. These Scripture statements in reference to the wonderful height and strength of these men *The giants of Bashan.* might be thought exaggerated; but the memorials of them, says Rev. J. L. Porter, are to be found in every section of Palestine in the form of graves of enormous dimensions. He personally examined, in his most interesting tour through Bashan, cities built and occupied by them forty centuries ago still in existence. "I have traversed," he says, "their streets, I have opened the doors of their houses, I have slept peacefully in their long-deserted halls. We shall see, too, that

[5] Sermons in the East, page 193.　　　[6] Num. xiii. 33.

106   THE WORD OF GOD OPENED.

among the massive ruins of these wonderful cities lie sculptured images of Astarte, with the crescent moon, which gave her the name of Carnaim, upon her brow."[7]

In the final conquest of Bashan, in the small province of Argob, it is said in Deuteronomy that Jair, one of the chiefs of the tribe of Manasseh, took no less than sixty great cities, The cities of Bashan. "fenced with high walls, gates, and bars, besides unwalled towns a great many."[8] Og, the last of the giants, whose bedstead was about fourteen feet in length and six in breadth, was the ruler of Bashan at this time. "Such a statement as this," says Porter, "seems all but incredible. It would not stand the arithmetic of Bishop Colenso for a moment. Often, when reading the passage, I used to think that some strange mystery hung over it, for What Porter saw in Bashan. how could a province measuring not more than thirty miles by twenty support such a number of fortified cities, especially when the greater part of it was a wilderness of rocks; but mysterious, incredible as this seemed, on the spot, with my own eyes, *I have seen* that it is literally true. The cities are there to this day. Some of them retain the ancient names recorded in the Bible."[9]

In these cities and the beautiful surrounding fields the tribes of Reuben, Gad, and the half tribe of Manasseh, naturally enough, desired to settle. "Bashan was regarded by Bashan in the poetry of the Bible. the prophets of Israel as an earthly paradise. The strength and grandeur of its oaks,[10] the beauty of its mountain scenery,[11] the unrivaled luxuriance of

---

[7] Giant Cities of Bashan, page 12.   [8] Deut. iii, 4, 5, 14.
[9] Giant Cities of Bashan, page 13.   [10] Ezek. xxvii, 6.   [11] Psa. lxxviii, 15.

its pastures,[12] the fertility of its wide-spreading plains, and the excellence of its cattle,[13] all supplied the sacred penmen with lofty imagery. Remnants of the oak forests still clothe the mountain side; the soil of the plains and the pastures on the downs are rich as of yore, and though the periodic raids of Arab tribes have greatly thinned the flocks and herds, as they have desolated the cities, yet such as remain—the rams and lambs, and goats and bulls—may be appropriately described in the words of Ezekiel as all of them fatlings of Bashan."[14] *Present appearance.*

In his very interesting travels in Arabia Petræa John L. Stephens, Esq., visited the wonderful but now vacant city of Petra, whose dwellings and temples and tombs, highly sculptured and ornamented, were scooped out of the sides of the mountain. *Stephens in Petra.* Upon this proud city of the descendants of Esau, in the mountains of Seir, because they refused to permit Israel to pass through their borders, the Almighty denounced the severest judgments. "I have sworn by myself, saith the Lord, that Bozrah (the strong or fortified city) shall become a desolation, a reproach, a waste, and a curse; and all the cities thereof shall be perpetual wastes. *Prophecies against Idumea.* Lo, I will make thee small among the heathen, and despised among men. Thy terribleness hath deceived thee, and the pride of thine heart, O thou that *dwellest in the clefts of the rocks*, that holdest the height of the hill: though thou shouldest make thy nest as high as the eagle, I will bring thee down from

---

[12] Jer. l, 19.   [13] Psa. xxii, 12; Micah vii, 14.
[14] Ezek. xxxix, 18. Giant Cities, pages 14, 15.

thence, saith the Lord."[15] "Thorns shall come up in her palaces, nettles and brambles in the fortresses thereof: and it shall be a habitation of dragons, and a court for owls."[16] "I would that the skeptic," says Stephens, "could stand as I did among the ruins of this city among the rocks, and there

The lesson to the skeptic. open the sacred book and read the words of the inspired penman, written when this desolate place was one of the greatest cities of the world. I see the scoffer arrested, his cheek pale, his lip quivering, and his heart quaking with fear as the ruined city cries out to him in a voice loud and powerful as that of one risen from the dead; though he would not believe Moses and the prophets he believes the handwriting of God himself in the desolation and eternal ruin around him."[17]

These illustrations will serve simply to indicate how valuable a service a knowledge of the geography and present condition of scriptural countries will render in the interpretation of Scripture. Our Christian literature is crowded with

Better reading than young people usually select valuable and interesting volumes of this description. If our young people would throw aside the unsubstantial and exciting tales and stories that come in avalanches from the press at the present time, and seek works of travel in their stead, they would soon acquire a taste and an appetite for what would nourish the intellect and quicken the spiritual life.

Customs and manners. III. It is necessary also to have some knowledge of the customs and manners of the people

---

[15] Jer. xlix, 13, 15. [16] Isa. xxxiv, 18.
[17] Travels in Egypt and Arabia Petræa, vol. ii, p. 58.

of the East. It is a curious fact that these customs to-day, in a large degree, are the same as those in Abraham's time. The Lord has permitted these habits to be stereotyped as a standing commentary upon and illustration of his word. Says Sir Samuel W. Baker, the celebrated English tourist, in his last volume, "The Nile Tributaries in Abys- *Testimony of Sir S. W. Baker.* sinia," referring to the customs of the native tribes, "this striking similarity to the descriptions of the Old Testament is exceedingly interesting to a traveler when residing among these curious and original people. With the Bible in one hand and these unchanged tribes before the eyes, there is a thrilling illustration of the sacred record; the past becomes the present; the vail of three thousand years is raised, and the living picture is a witness to the exactness of the historical description. At the same time there is a light thrown upon many obscure passages in the Old Testament by the experience of the present customs and figures of speech of the Arabs, which are precisely those that were practiced at the periods described."

The Song of Solomon, viewed in the light of our marriage service, which requires for its performance but a few moments, is incomprehensible, or can only *Song of Solomon.* be conceived of as a sensuous portrayal of marital love; but in the light of oriental custom, according to which the nuptial rites extended over a number of days, which were passed in delightful companionship, the longing of the Church for the coming of the bridegroom, the prophetic announcement of his approach, the joy in his presence, and also the panting of the individual soul for the "Chiefest among ten thousand," the grief at his delay, the holy ecstasy upon his approach, are all wonderfully illustrated in the protracted and elaborate ceremonies and triumphant choruses of an eastern marriage.

Several of the most impressive parables of our Lord require for their exposition, and the comprehension of their moral lessons, a knowledge of these rites. "What is written in the Bible must, as much as is needful, be placed more particularly in the light of the age from which it is descended, to which it alludes, and of which it speaks. We must pay attention to the civil, social, and religious conditions, ideas, and views with which that which is written stands in connection in any way."[18] There are but few chapters in the Bible for the clear understanding of which it is not necessary to be acquainted with the manners and customs of the East, in particular of the Jews, to be secured against misunderstanding.

Parables.

We must see what is written in the light of the times.

For illustration, the passage recorded in John i, 18, "which is in the bosom of the Father," referring to the near and unshared relation of the Son to the Father, is illustrated by their habit of reclining at the table. John, leaning next to his Master, reclined upon his bosom, and heard every word that dropped from his lips; so the only-begotten Son rested upon the bosom of the Father, and he only could reveal him and his word to the world. This custom, also, causing the limbs to be extended upon the couch behind them, illustrates the ease with which a grateful penitent could bathe the Saviour's feet while he sat at meat,

Illustrations of this.

---

[18] Manual of Hermeneutics. By Dr. Doedes. page 109.

wipe them with her disheveled hair, or anoint them with fragrant and precious ointment.[19]

The breaking of bread, which is referred to in Matt. xxvi, 26, and parallel passages, where it is said Jesus broke bread at the institution of the last supper, is a very natural thing, as those reclining at the table used no knives, and therefore bread had to be broken to be distributed. Very easily the expression came to signify the same as to eat, or to keep a feast.[20] "He who does not think of this, or does not know it, readily finds in that 'breaking of bread' a symbol, and that of the breaking of Jesus's body, which, however, was not broken. (See John xix, 33, 36.) In 1 Cor. xi, 24, the word 'broken' in the words of the institution of the Lord's supper does not belong to the original text."[21] It is omitted by Alford, Tischendorf, and others, in their editions of the Greek New Testament. These illustrations might readily be multiplied, but enough has been said to indicate the importance of the subject.

Breaking of bread.

Error as applied to Christ's body.

IV. The Bible is full of symbols. In all ages men have instinctively recognized in physical objects and events the outward expression of the thoughts and emotions of which they are conscious themselves, or of which they have perceived signs in others. "Thus the sun is the acknowledged emblem of power and creation, the tempest is a thunderbolt of wrath, the snow a symbol of purity, the rainbow of promise and hope. Spring-time and morning are symbols of youth, sunset and winter of age and death. The

Symbols

[19] Luke vii, 38; John xii, 3.   [20] Acts ii, 46; xx, 7.   [21] Dr. Doedes

mountains naturally suggest the idea of stability, and the sea that of immensity.[22] The lion is a symbol of fierceness, the lamb of innocence, the fox of cunning, the wolf of rapacity, and the dove of gentleness. In the Scriptures the horn is a symbol of strength and triumph, wings of swiftness, and eyes of intelligence. Hardly a page of Scripture can be found without a significant symbol. The ceremonial law was a collection of symbols. *The ceremonial law symbolical.* Of the divine symbols set forth in the costume of the priests, in the furniture of the tabernacle and temple, in the various sacrifices and festivals, the writer of the book of Hebrews gives a full exposition. We should not attempt to go further, as some do, with a 'zeal not according to knowledge,' and seek to find a spiritual meaning in the most trifling details of the Hebrew sanctuary: in the nails by which the *Symbols may be carried to extremes.* covering was fastened to the earth, in the golden snuffers, and in the tinkling bells upon the priestly robes. The writer heard a very earnest and very popular young divine, before a great body of Bible teachers, affirm that there was nothing, not even the simplest arrangement of the tabernacle, but had a spiritual application; which was simply nonsense. The author of the book of Hebrews shows that the Jewish service, taken as a whole, was a symbol of the Gospel, and was replete with a spiritual meaning *What Hebrews teaches* under material forms. It has been happily said that the best commentary upon the book of Leviticus is the Epistle to the Hebrews; and, what can be said of no other commentary, it is inspired. As a general principle, it may be

---

[22] Symbols of Christendom. By J. R. THOMPSON, M. A.

THE WORD OF GOD OPENED. 113

held unsafe to find any types in Old Testament characters, as Adam, Noah, Joseph, David, not affirmed to be such by the Scriptures themselves.

Throughout the Bible, numbers, unless it is definitely stated or clearly to be inferred that they are to be taken literally, are used symbolically. Seven is constantly used in this way to signify a complete or perfect number. Thus we read of seven lamps, seven stars, seven kings, seven diadems, seven hills, seven golden vials, seven angels, and seven spirits of God. The number twelve, as a complete number, we find multiplied into itself in the reckoning of the ransomed of Israel, who are estimated at one hundred and forty-four thousand. Forty means *many*. The city of Persepolis, in eastern language, is called "the city of forty towers," though the number is much larger. This is probably the meaning in 2 Kings viii, 9, where Hazael is said to have brought as a present to Elisha forty camels' burden of the good things of Damascus. Seventy is used to express a large, complete, but uncertain number. We are commanded to forgive till seventy times seven, to indicate that if our brother repent of his fault there must be no narrow limit to his forgiveness. The rude reckoning of a year was three hundred and sixty days; this multiplied by three and a half (a time, times, and half a time) gives twelve hundred and sixty, the famous prophetic and symbolic number which has given rise to so much conjecture. The Hebrew letters which form the word corresponding to "mystery" represent, when employed as numerals, the

Symbolical numbers.
The number seven.
Twelve.
Forty.
Seventy.
The three hundred and sixty days.
Six hundred and sixty-six

8

mystic number six hundred and sixty-six.[23] How astonishing that any one should build up a mathematical plan of the world's duration, upon such confessedly symbolical figures, of the exact value of which inspiration has given no measure.

Natural phenomena are constantly used as symbols in the Old and New Testaments. The sun is an emblem of glory and strength, the morning star of beauteous promise, the rainbow of God's covenant of mercy. In the Book of Revelation there are many symbols portending calamity, such as lightning and thunder, winds, fire and brimstone, the blackened sun, the blood-red moon, stars burning or falling from heaven, earthquake, fire, and flame.

Natural symbols.

Animals and their bodily members play a large part in the prophetical and poetical Scriptures. The four living ones ("beasts" in our version) of Ezekiel have given rise to volumes of controversy; they probably symbolize the whole animated creation. The white horse is the emblem of victory, the red of war, the black of famine, and the pale of death. The ferocity of the leopard and the bear, the headstrong push of the ram, the deadly bite of the scorpion, the destructiveness of locust-swarms, the deadly power of the serpent, furnish the key to their symbolic employment in prophecy.[24]

Animal symbols.

Jerusalem, the metropolis of the Land of Promise, and the place where the Lord especially recorded his name and manifested his presence, is often used to symbolize the Church of Christ in the ideal perfectness of her situation, economy, rule, and security On the other

Jerusalem and Babylon symbols of the Church.

[23] Symbols of Christendom.   [24] Ibid.

hand, Babylon, to the Jewish mind a name of ill omen, suggesting a memory of captivity, idolatry, and shame, is the personification of that sinful society which opposes and harasses the Church. The terms Sodom and Egypt, for the same reasons, are used for the same purpose.

The emblems of earthly royalty are freely employed in Scripture to denote the authority and reign of God and of created invisible powers. Many diadems upon one head denote plurality of dominion, which the pope of Rome still symbolizes in his triple crown or tiara. The iron scepter is the symbol of severity, as the Psalmist predicts: "He shall rule the nations with a rod of iron." The sword is the universal emblem of war; he who bears the sword is mighty to oppose and to subdue. "The sword going out of the mouth" is symbolical of the power attending the words of the august Speaker. *Earthly royalty.*

"The harvest and the vintage were, among the Jews, the chief seasons of agricultural festivity. In the symbolism of the Apocalypse, the corn harvest and the subsequent garnering denote the spiritual maturity and the eternal safety of Christ's people; the vintage, on the other hand, figures forth ripeness unto wrath; the treading of the grapes in the wine-press emblematizing the severity of the inevitable and divine vengeance. The sharp sickle is common to both, being the instrument in the one case of salvation, in the other of destruction. The vials which were emptied by the angels upon the earth were not what we understand by that term in English; they *The vintage and harvest.* *The vials.*

were the Latin *paterœ*, broad, flat bowls or dishes, used both in worship and in household affairs."[25] The harp is an

Harp, keys, and book. emblem of joy and praise; the scroll, or book, of purposes and decrees; the seal upon it denotes secresy. Keys signify power to admit and exclude; a gem or white stone, acquittal, friendship, or felicity. By eating a book, or scroll, is intended participation in the divine purposes; by drinking the wine of wrath and the cup of vengeance, the enduring of the divine displeasure.

The bride. The bride is the pure, chosen, and beloved Church of Christ. The Church is also represented under the similitude of the woman clothed with the sun. The harlot is the idolatrous, antichristian body tempting the true Church to forsake the Lord.[26]

The great battle between truth and error is set forth in the

Battle of Armageddon. Revelation in symbols taken from the prophecy of Ezekiel, in which the forces of Gog and Magog represent the combined hosts of error gathered from every quarter. Of its final result the Church of Christ is left in no anxious doubt. It often occurs in the Old Testament that the prophets predict the judgments which God is about

Symbolical acts. to visit upon the nations by symbolical acts, as where Isaiah is directed to "loose the sackcloth from his loins," to "put off the shoe from his foot," and he is

Walking naked and barefoot said to have done so "walking naked and barefoot three years a sign and a wonder."[27] Evidently this was not actually done by the prophet, for it would have been a shameful exposure of his person; but the

[25] J. R. Thompson.   [26] Ibid.   [27] Isa. xx.

symbolic picture is presented, illustrating the judgments of God about to be brought upon Egypt and Ethiopia. Ere long they would be conquered in battle, made captives, and be led forth "naked and barefoot, even with their buttocks uncovered, to the shame of Egypt." Thus by this pictured symbol a *shameful uncovering* or a disgraceful humiliation of the proud idolatrous powers upon whom Israel was inclined to lean for support in her threatened invasions from the East, is pointed out. If the prophet had simply exposed himself in this manner no one would have connected his shame with that of the designated countries; or, if he had declared this, his constant appearance for three years would have utterly destroyed its impressiveness. It was simply a symbolized prophecy. <small>Symbolical only, or without force.</small>

Thus also the symbolical marriage of the prophet to the prophetess,[26] and the birth of a son with a symbolic name, could not have been a literal occurrence, because such a course would have been simply adultery, as evidently the prophetess was not of his family. The object of the prophetic warning was to show the Jewish people that a certain overthrow would be speedily visited upon the combined powers of Samaria and Damascus. For this purpose the prophet is led by God to the prophetess, that by the conjunction of a twofold prophetical character in the parentage there might be a birth in the strongest sense prophetical. The name of the child is significant as translated: *hasten, spoil, quick prey.* Before the predictive child should be able to cry "My father," God declares by Isaiah, that both Syria <small>Marriage of the prophet to the prophetess.</small>

[26] Isaiah viii, 1-31.

and Damascus shall have fallen under the stroke of Assyria. As a predictive symbol, the prophecy is impressive; as an actual fact, it would have been inconsistent, criminal, and without power to awaken conviction.[29]

These illustrations will afford aid in the consideration of many symbolical prophecies which, literally understood, shock the moral sense, but considered simply as picturesque and significant signs are striking and full of force. "Hosea," for example, "is commanded to marry two impure women; *Symbols of Hosea and Ezekiel.* Ezekiel to lie on his left side three hundred and ninety days, looking at an iron pan, then turn over to his right side, on which he must lie forty additional days, eating during the whole period a compost of lentiles, beans, barley, millet, and fitches, prepared in a manner most decidedly offensive. We affirm boldly that the expositors who consider these, and others which might be mentioned, as real transactions, dishonor the word of God, while they betray a want of taste that is astounding. Beyond all doubt, they were symbolical representations that passed before the prophet's mind in his inspired ecstasy." [30]

It will be seen how modestly and carefully these scriptural symbols must be used. Many enthusiastic symbolists have *Symbols should be interpreted with great care.* staked their reputation upon views of the future depending upon their proper rendering of these often mysterious symbols, and have been terribly abased by the result. What is distinctly revealed is for us and our children; but what God has seen fit to vail we are to receive as indistinct disclosures of divine purposes, held out as great

---

[29] Fairbairn on Prophecy, page 501.   [30] Canon and Interpretation, page 205

but distant lights for the direction and encouragement of the Church.

V. We will refer to but one other preliminary requisite to the safe interpretation of the holy records, and that is, that we should endeavor to be in sympathy in thought and feeling with the sacred writers. This is necessary in reference to any ancient or foreign author. "Language," says Fairbairn, "is but the utterance of thought and feeling on the part of one person to another, and the more we can identify ourselves with the state of mind out of which that thought and feeling arose the more manifestly shall we be qualified for appreciating the language in which they are embodied, and reproducing true and living impressions of it." [31]

<small>Must be in sympathy with sacred writers.</small>

Thus Hagenbach remarks in his Encyclopedia, "An inward interest in the doctrine of theology is needful for a biblical interpreter. As we say that a philosophical spirit is demanded for the study of Plato, a poetical taste for the reading of Homer or Pindar, a sensibility to wit and satire for the perusal of Lucian, a patriotic sentiment for the enjoyment of Sallust and Tacitus, equally certain is it that fitness to understand the profound truths of Scripture presupposes, as an indispensable requisite, a sentiment of piety, an inward religious experience." The excellent Neander's motto was, "*Pectus est quod theologium facit:*" "It is the heart that makes the theology." It is the want of this living sympathy and divine experience that renders certain, otherwise so intelligent, scholars blind

<small>Hagenbach upon inward interest.</small>

<small>Motto of Neander.</small>

---

[31] Hermeneutical Manual, page 80.

to the significant meaning of the Scriptures. The learned but rationalistic Dr. Paulus, of Heidelberg, upon the passage, "Blessed art thou, for flesh and blood have not revealed it to thee, but my Father that is in heaven," can see nothing more than a reference to the force of circumstances in awakening the mind toward what is good; and in the words, "I must work the works of Him that sent me while it is day; the night cometh when no man can work;" all the sense he can find is, "I must heal the diseased eyes before the evening twilight comes on, because when it is dark we can no longer see to work."[32]

Dr. Paulus.

Thus it ever has been, and always will be, as Jesus said when upon earth, "Thou hast hid these things from the wise and prudent, and revealed them unto babes."

What Jesus said.

"When the Christian reads," says Dr. Stowe, "what Jesus said to Martha, '*one thing is needful*,' his own Christian consciousness teaches him that true religion, the love of Christ, is here meant as the one thing needful, and both grammar and lexicography sustain his position; but Paulus, who has no Christian consciousness, in the proper sense of the term, can see in these words nothing more than a declaration from the intellectual and temperate Rabbi to the anxious woman cumbered about much serving, and eager to prepare a sumptuous entertainment for her beloved teacher, that *one dish is enough for supper*, nor can grammar and lexicon alone prove the interpretation to be wrong."[33]

Dr. Goulburn starts the inquiry why the Bible offers so

[32] Dr. Fairbairn.   [33] Bibliotheca Sacra

little attraction to most persons, and why they seem to gather their theological views from any other source rather than the Bible, and answers it thus: "It is, I fear, that we are interested in theology, and not in religion; in questions and controversies rather than in godly edifying which is in faith. Our *minds* are interested, and we read religious works to feed and stimulate them. Our *hearts* are comparatively uninterested, and so the light of the heart, the food of the heart, the joy of the heart, the comfort of the heart, are reckoned cheap and common things in our eyes." We need the presence and inward aid of the Holy Spirit in order clearly to apprehend revealed truth, "for what man knoweth the things of a man save the spirit of man which is in him? even so the things of God knoweth no man, but the Spirit of God."[34] The Scriptures cannot be deeply and perfectly understood except by the guidance of the same mind which inspired them. The letter of the Scriptures may be familiar to us from our youth upward, but to God's own thought and counsel we shall be strangers until the Holy Spirit, by his divine communications, reveals them to our souls. Dr. Goulburn happily illustrates this truth by comparing the Bible to a sun-dial, which is in itself perfect and complete, graven with all the hours, and with a gnomon or index, which casts an exact shadow; but what avails a sun-dial without light? On a cloudy day, in the twilight, or at midnight, it cannot inform us of the time; so the Bible is the chart of life, and is "able to make us wise

Answer to query why so little interest in the Bible?

Men need the Holy Spirit.

The Inspirer of the Scripture must enlighten us.

This truth illustrated.

---
[34] 1 Cor. ii, 11.

unto salvation;" but its one indispensable condition is, that the Spirit, while we are reading it, shall be shining upon the heart. The Psalmist seems to have regard to this double necessity when he prays, "O send out thy *light* and thy *truth*, that they may lead me and bring me to thy holy hill!"

Prayer of the Psalmist.

To guard against any misapprehension of the character of this work of the Holy Spirit enlightening the mind in answer to prayer, it is proper to remark that one is not to expect after he has prayed "any sudden influx of a wonderful light, quite distinct from the ordinary powers of reflection and memory. The Holy Spirit acts upon the mind *through* the ordinary mental faculties, not without them, or independently of them. When, after careful, patient, and prayerful thought, or after an effort of the imagination to realize some scriptural narrative in all its details, we find that the difficulties, one after another, begin to clear up, like clouds rolling away from the bosom of a mountain, and revealing patches of verdure smitten with the sunbeam; or when memory recalls some apposite allusion elsewhere, or some illustrative experience, through which we ourselves have passed—the light so vouchsafed is undistinguishable in our consciousness from that which is supplied by our natural faculties; it is supplied *through* them, they being called into operation and assisted by grace, whose primary actings are in the abyssmal depths of the mind, far beyond the ken of the keenest self-intuition."[35]

Nature of this work of the Spirit.

Spirit acts through the mind.

[35] Devotional Study of the Scriptures.

Whatever other source of information may be beyond the teacher's reach in entering upon the work of interpreting Scripture, this highest source of spiritual illumination is ever open and ever available, for saith our Lord, "If ye then, being evil, know how to give good gifts unto your children, how much more shall your heavenly Father give the Holy Spirit to them that ask him."[36]

This grace always proffered to us.

[36] Luke xi, 13.

CHAPTER VI.

RULES OF INTERPRETATION.

RULE I.

THE literal meaning is to be given to all words, unless it will cause them to express what is inconsistent with universal experience as to the nature of things, or with the declared opinions of the sacred writers in other passages, or at variance with the evident scope of the passage itself.

Always recollecting that the Scriptures are for the most part written in the language of common life, unless we find *Obvious meaning the true one.* positive qualifying reasons apparent the obvious and common-sense significance of the language of the sacred writers is to be received as the true meaning. We are not to apply a sense to the words that will best suit our opinion of what should have been said, or what we desire should be said; but our only inquiry is, What *did* *Bengel on holding to Scripture text.* they say? Bengel was accustomed to say, "It is better to run all lengths with Scripture truth in a natural and open manner than to shift and twist and accommodate. Every single truth is a light of itself, and every error, however minute, is darkness as far as it goes."[1]

---

[1] Of the various opinions that have been forced upon the simple utterances of Scripture Dr. Stowe remarks: "As an illustration of this, read such works

Melanchthon, the St. John of the Reformation in spirit, and its scholar in literature, says in his Elements of Rhetoric, "The sense of Scripture is one, certain, and simple, and is every where to be ascertained in accordance with the principles of grammar and human discourse." *Melanchthon.*

The reformer himself says, with characteristic earnestness: "We must not make God's word mean what we wish; we must not bend *it*, but allow it to bend *us;* and give it the honor of being better than we could make it, so that we must let it stand." *Martin Luther.*

The simplest and most natural meaning that flows from

as Owen on the Hebrews, or M'Knight on the Epistles. Able books in their way, and showing no small amount of intellectual acumen and industrious scholarship; but how many things they think of, how many arguments they have, how much meaning they will find in Paul, at which the apostle himself would be astonished with great astonishment if he knew it were attributed to him! The same is true of some of the purest and strongest of our New England writers. If Moses and Isaiah and David and John and Paul had been natives of New England, habituated to the New England modes of thought, educated in New England colleges, and settled ministers over New England parishes, these expositions of our excellent fathers would have been very correct; but as matters are, they in many cases rather project themselves than expound the sacred writers. Dr. Burton, in his proof-texts for the *Taste Scheme*, has the most comforting conviction that the apostle Paul was full of the same philosophy with himself; and Dr. Emmons, in his Scriptural proofs of the *Exercise Scheme*, has the most unflinching assurance that the apostle Paul was clearly and heartily an exerciser; but I suspect the apostle would be greatly surprised to learn that he was either the one or the other, and as much confounded if the question were put to him which he was, as if he were asked whether he were a Lockeian or a Coleridgeite. Those questions were not up in his day, nor did the apostle's reasoning run on those lines. You might as well start the question whether he journeyed from Miletus to Jerusalem on a railroad or in a steamboat, and adduce long and learned arguments in favor of one of these hypotheses and against the other."—*Bibliotheca Sacra*, vol. x, p. 48.

the words, giving the least impression of constraint or uncommon use, may, other things being equal, be relied upon as the sense in which the words are to be understood. The writers were from comparatively humble ranks in life. "Their manners and habits, their modes of conception and forms of speech, are such as usually belong to persons similarly circumstanced; that is, they partake, not of the polish and refinement, the art and subtlety, which too commonly mark the footsteps of high cultivation and luxurious living, but of the free, the open, the natural, as of persons accustomed frankly to express, not to conceal, their emotions, or to wrap their sentiments in disguise."[2]

The simplest meaning the true one.

The writers men of humble origin.

REMARK 1. *Where, however, the literal meaning asserts that which is known to be impossible it must be given up; it is evidently then a symbolical or figurative expression.* As, for illustration, when the psalmist says, "The wicked are estranged from the womb; they go astray as soon as they be born, speaking lies."[3] The literal meaning is impossible here, for no one can *speak* lies from the moment of birth; while the truth taught, that the depraved heart from the first leads the unregenerate person astray, is readily understood. In Jeremiah's prophecy we read, "They have sown wheat, but shall reap thorns."[4] Wheat seed would never be followed by a harvest of thorns; but the expectation which they cherished of a bountiful and wholesome return from their labors would be blasted.

When literal meaning asserts an impossibility it must be given up.

"When it is said in 1 Cor. xv, 22, 'For as in Adam all

[2] Fairbairn's Hermeneutical Manual.   [3] Psa. lviii, 3.   [4] Jer. xii, 13.

the, even so in Christ shall all be made alive,' these words, *as in Adam all die*, cannot be intended to affirm that all men existed in Adam, nor that they all sinned in his person, nor that they all died when he died. These are known impossibilities. One person cannot be all mankind; all mankind cannot be one person. Men cannot exist before they exist; they cannot die before they live; they cannot sin before they act."[b] Some other meaning, therefore, which the Scriptures themselves would naturally afford, must be found for this expression. So when, in Matthew x, 34, Christ tells his disciples that "he came not to send peace on earth, but a sword," no justification from the literal rendering can be found for the violent persecution of those esteemed to be Christ's enemies; but history interprets clearly its meaning. The Gospel has ever occasioned differences and discords in families and nations by inducing some to accept its self-denying truth; while others have rejected it, and have bitterly opposed its friends. Illustration from 1 Cor. xv. 22.

Christ sending a "sword" upon earth no justification of persecution.

"When David says that 'he is poured out like water, and all his bones are out of joint; that his heart is melted in the midst of his bowels,' we perceive instantly that a literal pouring out and melting cannot be meant, as nothing of the kind has ever been witnessed. When the Redeemer, in the institution of the supper, declares of the bread that it is his body, and of the wine that it is his blood, we necessarily understand him to be speaking figuratively and symbolically. My

David "poured out like water."

The bread and wine in the sacrament.

[b] Doble.

senses distinctly see, taste, smell, and feel that the sacramental elements are nothing but real bread and wine. If the Scriptures really taught the Popish doctrine of transubstantiation they would declare a falsehood, which would be quite sufficient by itself to destroy their authority. If my senses may deceive me, how shall I convince myself that I ever saw a book called the Bible, or read it, or ever heard of such a being as Jesus Christ." [6]

Thus says the spiritual and learned Augustine, a bishop of the Church before it became corrupted, upon the passage in St. John's Gospel in reference to eating the flesh and drinking the blood of Christ: "It appears to order a wicked and abominable action; it is, therefore, a figure teaching that we must communicate with our Lord's passion, and have it sweetly and properly laid up in our memory that his flesh was crucified and wounded for us."

Augustine on the body and blood.

We may readily decide whether a passage is figurative or literal by asking the question: If the words are taken just as they stand, will the idea expressed be true, or contrary to experience and the nature of things?

How to know a figurative expression.

When Jesus calls his disciples his sheep, we cannot doubt that, by a significant figure, he suggests his affection for them and his care of them, and their confidence in and attachment to him; and, also, the qualities of temper and character that he expects to find in them. Thus, sin is called in Scripture a debt; atonement, the payment of a debt; pardon, the forgiveness of a debt. These are not literal terms, but figures of speech suggesting spiritual

The disciples the "sheep" of Jesus.

[6] M'Lelland.

truths. We may not hold these terms to a rigid construction, and maintain that because Christ died *for* man's sin, therefore all will be finally saved; or, that because he has obeyed the law, therefore sinners are free to live in sin. Men are represented in the Bible to be dead in sin, but they are not dead in such a sense as to be unable to see and feel the truth; neither are they free from the duty of repentance; nor are they guiltless if they disregard the divine call. More errors, probably, have arisen from pushing figurative expressions to an extreme than from any other single cause; and against this tendency the sober, earnest student of the Bible needs to be specially on his guard.⁷ <small>These figures must not be rigidly construed.</small>

The difficulty in understanding a figurative passage is sometimes readily resolved by referring to parallel passages which treat of the same subject under other symbols or in literal terms, or to the context. Thus in the inimitable Sermon upon the Mount, the first beatitude is a benediction upon the *poor*, according to the Gospel of St. Luke, while in St. Matthew's Gospel its meaning is clearly interpreted in the additional phrase, <small>Figures interpreted by parallel passages. The first beatitude.</small> "Blessed are the poor *in spirit*," which plainly indicates the error of the Romanists in their enforced poverty in their orders of mendicant Monks, and the real virtue commended— consciousness of spiritual necessities, the opposite of spiritual pride. Dr. Fairbairn applies this principle to 1 Cor. iii, 13, which declares that every man's work shall be made manifest, being revealed by fire:—"The declaration here made," he says, "is, that 'the day,' namely, of coming

<small>⁷ Bible Hand-Book: Angus.</small>

trial, 'shall be revealed by fire, and the fire shall try every man's work of what sort it is.' What is the nature of the work to be tried? (as revealed in the context.) This is naturally the first question. Is it of a moral, or simply of an external and earthly kind? The only work spoken of in the context is that which concerns the progress of Christ's Church, and man's relation to it — work, therefore, in a strictly moral sense; and so the fire that is to try it must be moral too. For how incongruous were it to couple a corporeal fire with a spiritual service, as the means of determining its real character!" If we have recourse to other passages which speak of future trial, we find, indeed, that the Lord will be revealed in flaming fire; but as to what shall really fix the character and the award of each man's work in the Lord, we are left in no room to doubt that it shall be his own searching judgment: this it is that shall bring all clearly to light.[e]

Dr. Fairbairn on 1 Cor iii, 13, "revealed by fire," as illustrated by context.

REMARK 2. *We may be assured, if the letter of any Scripture seems to violate our moral sense, or to contradict another moral precept, it cannot be intended to have its ordinary sense.* When Christ says, "If any man hate not his father, and mother, and wife, and children, he cannot be my disciple," he does not intend to teach us that we must break the fourth commandment. Every human instinct which God has implanted in the heart would revolt against such a rendering. Christ simply uses the strongest earthly figure to express our supereminent obligation to him. As much as we rightly love our

The meaning must not contradict moral sense.

What Christ intended by hating father and mother.

[e] Fairbairn's Hermeneutical Manual, p. 163.

parents, we should love him more. Nothing but duty to Christ can come between the perfect obedience of the child to the reasonable commands of a parent.

A literal rendering of the command in Matt. xviii, 9, "to cut off the right hand and pluck out the right eye," would be a breach of the spirit of the sixth commandment; while Christ simply teaches that whatever stands between a soul and its duty, as revealed by the Holy Spirit, is to be surrendered, even if the self denial is as painful as the loss of an eye or a hand. "Put a knife to thy throat, if thou be a man given to appetite," as written in Prov. xxiii, 2, is not an exhortation to suicide, but a warning against gluttony. *Cutting off the hand.*

"In Luke x, 4 Christ commands his disciples 'not to salute (during one of their missionary journeys) any by the way,' a precept which our Quaker brethren obey to the letter. But Christ could never have intended to inculcate rudeness; it must therefore mean, 'Do not lose time by holding unnecessary intercourse with your friends; use all expedition in journeying to the scene of your labors.' Equally absurd is their well-known exposition of the precept, 'when smitten on the one cheek, turn the other also,' as if our Saviour disapproved of self-defense."[9] *Figurative precepts.*

In Rom. v, 19 we read, "For as by one man's disobedience many were made sinners, so by the obedience of one shall many be made righteous." If we interpret this verse literally we are at once forced to trample upon our moral intuitions as to right and wrong. We *Many made sinners.*

[9] M'Lelland.

cannot force our moral natures to admit the justice of *making* men sinners, on account of the sin of another, without their knowledge or consent. "Such a sense is contrary to the known nature of man as a free agent. That nature is such that he cannot be made a sinner but by his own personal and voluntary choice. Besides, the terms of justification through the merits of Christ are such that no man can partake of its benefits save by a personal and voluntary faith in him. If, therefore, men are not made righteous through Christ except on condition of their voluntary faith, neither, in all fairness, are they made sinners through Adam except on condition of their breaking the divine law through the free choice of their own wills. Whatever meaning, therefore, may be affixed to the passage it must be one that shall consist with the nature of man and with the nature of sin, for it is a primary principle that the Scriptures every where speak in harmony with the nature of the objects of which they treat." [10]

The Bible does not draw nice theological and metaphysical distinctions. The apostle simply teaches that as our moral nature is overthrown and disorganized through our descent from a fallen and sinful man, and moral beings from their first volitions are sinful, so that moral nature is restored and sanctified by the coming into it of the Lord Jesus. When he is admitted into the heart the lost balance is restored, and the acts are righteous.

<small>What the apostle teaches.</small>

<small>Christ made sin for us.</small> Of the same class is the Scripture found in 2 Cor. v, 21, "For he hath made him to be sin

[10] Doble.

for us, who knew no sin." Here would be a positive contradiction to all the known nature of things if the words were taken literally. Our sinless Lord could not by any possibility be made to be sin. He is made, however, to be a *sin offering*—an expiatory sacrifice for our sin—so that we, penitently trusting in him, may be accounted as if we were righteous before God.

The passage in Prov. xvi, 4, where it is said, "The Lord hath made all things for himself; yea, even the wicked for the day of evil," has been thought by some to teach the forbidding doctrine that the wicked were created that they might be condemned; but this would be contrary to every conviction of justice, and to manifold other Scriptures, such as Psa. cxlv, 9; Ezek. xviii, 23; 2 Peter iii, 9. The meaning, therefore, must be that all evil shall in some way contribute to the glory of God, and promote the accomplishment of his will. *The wicked made for the day of evil.*

There are many things that the Bible reveals which transcend human thought, but nothing contradictory to the moral nature which God has given us if it comes within the bounds of our knowledge and experience. No man is required to do injustice to his enlightened convictions of right and wrong by any requisition which the sacred record makes upon his faith or practice. *Nothing contradictory to moral convictions.*

REMARK 3. *When the literal interpretation is contrary to universal experience its meaning must be modified;* as when a passage of Scripture states absolutely what is a general truth, but has often exceptions. *When contrary to universal experience must be modified.*

Thus Solomon says in Prov. xxii, 6, "Train up a child in

Training of a child. the way he should go, and when he is old he will not depart from it." This is not always true. The verse means this is the tendency of such training, although the apparent exceptions, after all, may be very often attributed to some failure in parental training even in the case of very devoted and estimable persons. In

A soft answer. Prov. xv, 1 it is said, "A soft answer turneth away wrath." This *is* its tendency, although certainly in every case this is not the result. And so when Paul declares that

The goodness of God. the "goodness of God leadeth to repentance," he states a general truth. This is its inclination; but how many resist it to their own destruction! So, also, when we are commanded by our Lord to "take no thought

Taking no thought, and praying without ceasing. for the morrow," and by the apostle to "pray without ceasing," the natural modifications of the literal signification of the words are so evident that no one can fail to perceive them. In John i, 11, 12 it is said,

His own received him not. "He came unto his own, and his own received him not." It might seem from this that not one of his own nation received him. The next sentence, however, suggests the scriptural modification, "But as many as received him," comparatively few received him.

REMARK 4. We shall consider in another chapter the interpretation of the poetic books, and of prophecy. Nothing can be more evident than that the latter cannot be understood literally. Hundreds have attempted it. Sys-

Interpreting prophecy must not be literal. tems of hermeneutics have been prepared purporting to give the exact significance of prophetic symbols. In our own country incalculable evil has been brought upon the cause of Christ; especially upon local Churches and individuals led away by the sincere but mistaken opinions of teachers who have ventured upon a literal rendering of prophecy.

These are the natural exceptions, arising out of the idioms and customs of speaking of the times, to the principle of the rule, but in no measure affecting its value as a broad canon for our guidance in the interpretation of the sacred writings.

Rule II.

In settling the meaning of words we must have respect chiefly to the current sense or established usage at the time they were uttered, rather than to their etymology.

The importance of this rule is obvious even in the interpretation of a book written in our own language two or three hundred years since. Thus the word *villain*, which at the present time signifies an extremely depraved person, formerly meant the poor serf attached to the villa or farm of a proprietor. As they were ignorant, and generally dishonest and dissolute, when the original relation ceased, the term was applied to such a character as they were accustomed to exhibit. In our English version of the Scriptures we find the word *let*, which now signifies to permit, used as it formerly was in the sense of hindering.[11]

The term *prevent*, now usually signifies to restrain, but in

Changes in our own language.

[11] Romans I, 13.

the Scripture it often has its appropriate meaning, as derived from the Latin, to come before, or to anticipate. Thus the psalmist says: "But unto thee have I cried, O Lord; and in the morning shall my prayer *prevent* (or come before) thee."[12] An Englishman speaks of a man as *clever*, meaning that he is capable, dexterous; while we generally use the term as expressing amiableness and good nature.

In Gal. vi, 2 we are directed to "bear one another's burdens, and so fulfill the law of Christ;" while immediately *As to bearing our own and others' burdens.* after, in the fifth verse, we are told that "every one shall bear his own burden." The context throws some light upon the different uses of the same term, indicating that one is the burden of one's trials and infirmities, which may readily be shared in by others, while the other is the burden of his personal responsibility, or the burden of his personal state and destiny, which he must bear himself alone. In the original terms used to express these two burdens the difference is at once seen. The burdens which we are to bear for one another are expressed by a Greek word signifying the *weights*, the things which press like loads upon those who come in contact with them; but the burden which each one is to bear for himself is expressed by two words which signify *his own baggage*, the solemn personal accountability which God has laid upon him. Dr. Fairbairn gives an interesting illustration of this rule in the interpretation of 2 Cor. xii, 9. The apostle here says that he *The import of "the power of Christ resting upon one."* would most willingly rather glory in infirmities, "that the power of Christ may rest upon me,"

---

[12] Psalm lxxxviii, 13.

which sentence but imperfectly presents the force and signification of the original. The verb employed, translated *may rest*, belongs to the later Greek, and is found in Polybius in the sense of dwelling in a tent, or inhabiting. The word, however, can only be explained by referring to what is said in the Old Testament Scriptures (which was familiar to the apostle) of the relation of the Lord's tabernacle or tent to his people; for example, as where it is written in Isa. iv, 6, "And there shall be a tabernacle for a shadow in the daytime from the heat," signifying the Lord's gracious presence and protection spread over them as a shelter. So, also, in Rev. vii, 15 the Lord is represented as "tabernacling upon" the redeemed in glory. In like manner the apostle here states it as the reason why he would rejoice in infirmities, that thereby Christ's power might tabernacle upon him—might serve him, so to speak, as the abiding refuge and divine resort in which he could hide himself.

Archbishop Leighton calls attention to the expressive word used to denote God's opposition to the proud. God *resisteth* the proud; sets himself in battle array (for this is the force of the word) against pride, as if it were his grand enemy.[13]

<small>God resisting the proud.</small>

The Jews frequently expressed a qualifying thought by the use, not of an adjective, but of a second noun, a practice which is also seen in the Hebrew Greek of the New Testament. In 2 Cor. i, 5 Paul says, the "sufferings of Christ abound in us." This is a very common idiom of the Scriptures. It means, not the sufferings experienced by Christ himself, but

[13] Fairbairn's Hermeneutical Manual.

those which we suffer for him. Thus, when the apostle calls himself a prisoner of Christ, he means that he was imprisoned for his belief in Christ. In various chapters of Romans Paul speaks of the "righteousness of God," by which he plainly signifies, not the excellency of the divine nature, but the righteousness by which the sinner is justified, and which he calls God's righteousness, because he graciously provided the means of its attainment, and accepts it. All this is in accordance with the Hebrew idiom, which employs the genitive (or possessive case) in the place of an adjective, as where the apostle speaks of the "patience of hope" for *patient hope*, the "glory of his power" for *his glorious power*.

<small>Hebraisms.</small>

Things are sometimes said to be done which are only attempted, or where there is an endeavor or desire to do them. Reuben is said to "have delivered Joseph out of the hands of his brethren." He sought to do so, although he failed in his purpose. "Whoso findeth his life," says our Saviour, "shall lose it," that is, seeks to find or save it—is unduly anxious—at the expense of duty. Sometimes an act is said to be done by a person when he is simply the *occasion* of it. Thus Jeremiah declares (xxxviii, 23) that God says to the unhappy king Zedekiah, that he shall be taken by the hand of the king of Babylon, and shall "cause Jerusalem to be burnt with fire." The conduct of Zedekiah led to this mournful result at the hand of the king of Babylon. He did not order Jerusalem to be burned, but it was burned on his account. This explains the apparent discrepancy between Matthew's and Luke's account of the purchase of the "field of blood."

<small>Things said to be done which are only attempted.</small>

<small>One who occasions an act said to do it.</small>

The former states that it was bought by the priests and elders with the money that Judas returned to them; the latter, in Acts i, 18, says: "This man [Judas] purchased a field with the reward of iniquity." In this case he was the occasion of the purchase, and according to the current habit of speech, was said to have made it himself.

That which is difficult or inconvenient or unjust was often said to be impossible, as when in Ruth iv, 6, the kinsman of Elimelech says, "I *cannot* redeem his inheritance." He had property enough to do it, but it was inconvenient for him to assume the necessary obligations. When the householder in our Lord's parable was called at midnight to give admission to a friend, he replies: "The door is shut, the children are with me in bed, and I cannot rise and give." He means, it would be a great discomfort for him to do so. So, when in Mark vi, 5 it is said of our Lord that "he could there do no mighty work because of their unbelief," it is meant that he could not consistently or justly, or from the fact that their unbelief kept them from coming to him so that he might save them. *(Things said to be impossible.)*

This suggestion will aid in the understanding of that large class of Scriptures which refer to God as causing us to "err from" his "ways," "hardening" our "hearts," "shutting the eyes" of sinners, and making their "ears heavy," lest they "should see with their eyes and hear with their ears." What God has in wisdom and in love *permitted*, or what has occurred in the operation of laws which he has established, he is said, in this familiar idiom, to have done. He "hardened Pharaoh's heart," by permitting him to *(Explains passages which refer human acts to God.)*

harden himself through neglect of those very means which serve, when properly improved, to soften and subdue the affections.

Sometimes the names of parents or ancestors are used in the Scriptures for their posterity. Thus in Gen. ix, 25, it is written, "Cursed be Canaan;" but the curse fell not upon himself; it rested upon his sinful posterity. This curse, it should be recollected, did not rest upon his righteous descendants, for both Melchisedek and Abimelech were Canaanites, as was the woman who came to Christ, and whose daughter was healed.[14] In the same way Jacob and Israel are often put for the Israelites, as in Psa. xiv, 7. The word "son" is often used in reference to a remote ancestor, as the priests were called the sons of Levi.

The parents' names used for descendants.

Brother means a relative. *Brother* is used in the same way, as referring to any collateral relation. Abraham applies the term to Lot, who was his nephew. Jair is called the son of Manasseh, because his grandfather had married the daughter of one of the heads of Manasseh. Mary, the mother of our Lord, is also thought to have descended from David in this way, so that our Lord was David's son, not only through his reputed father, but by direct descent through his mother. Modern biblical scholars suppose Joseph and Mary to have been distant relatives. In 2 Kings viii, 26 Athaliah is called the daughter of Omri, while in the eighteenth verse of the same chapter she is called the daughter of Ahab. She was Ahab's daughter and Omri's granddaughter.

These illustrations simply indicate the importance of this

---

[14] Genesis xiv, 18; xx, 6; Matthew xv, 22–28.

rule, and will suggest to the young interpreter the value of a good critical commentary to give him the exact meaning of Scripture terms according to the *usus loquendi*, the current sense, of the times in which they were uttered. Value of critical notes.

Rule III.

To the utmost extent that it can be secured by reference to parallel passages, and especially to the context and other portions of Scripture written by the same sacred penman, the Bible should be made its own expositor.

By parallel passages are meant those teaching the same doctrine, or relating the same facts; passages of the Old Testament alluded to in the New, as illustrations, or as prophecies fulfilled; portions of the Scriptures where the same terms are used under other circumstances, showing the various significations given by the sacred writers to the terms they use. Our reference Bibles, one of which should always be in the hands of a teacher, have accumulated a valuable collection of collated texts. But much will remain for the Bible scholar himself to do in this direction. Many of the passages in a reference Bible have but the most remote, if any, relation to the Scripture they are said to be the parallel of, and many more a diligent student will collate by the aid of the concordance for his own benefit. It is wonderful how, in skillful hands, the Bible can be made to pour inspired light upon its own difficult passages.

Parallel passages.

Reference Bible.

"I will not scruple to assert," says the learned Bishop Horsley, "that the most illiterate Christian, if he can but read his English Bible, and will take the pains to read it in this manner (studying the parallel passages) without any other commentary than what the different parts mutually furnish for each other, will not only attain all that practical knowledge which is necessary to salvation, but will become learned in every thing relating to his religion in such a degree that he will not be liable to be misled, either by the refuted arguments or the false assertions of those who endeavor to engraft their own opinions upon the oracles of God. He may safely be ignorant of all philosophy and all history which he does not find in the sacred books."

Bishop Horsley upon comparison of Scriptures.

It is by comparing Scripture with Scripture that we become sure of the true meaning of particular passages, and especially are able to ascertain the doctrines of the Bible on questions of faith and practice. "A Scripture truth is really the consistent explanation of all that Scripture teaches in reference to the question to be examined, and a Scripture duty is the consistent explanation of all the precepts of Scripture on the duty examined. It is in studying the Scriptures as in studying the works of God. We first examine each fact or phenomenon, and ascertain its meaning, and then classify it with other similar facts, and attempt to explain the whole."[15] From not studying their sacred books in this way the Jews made their great mistake in rejecting

In this way find the true meaning of Scripture doctrine.

Error of the Jews.

[15] Angus.

Christ. "We have heard out of the law," they say, "that Christ abideth forever:" (this truth had been revealed in Isa. ix, 7, and in Daniel vii, 14:) "and how sayest thou," they inquire, that "the Son of man must be lifted up?" The Messiah's everlasting kingdom had indeed been foretold, but it had also been prophesied that he should be "brought as a lamb to the slaughter," and that he should be "cut off, though not for himself." [16]

Great wisdom must be used in interpreting the spiritual references in the New Testament to the ritual services of the Old. In such passages as distinctly exhibit the differences between the New and the Old, it is the *differences* which are to be chiefly insisted upon; while in those passages which present Christian privileges and duties under the symbols of the Old Testament, the agreement should be specially dwelt upon.

<small>Care must be had in spiritualizing the sacred rites of the Old Testament.</small>

Thus when the apostle, in the twelfth of Romans, enjoins a living sacrifice, there is a significant harmony shown between the two dispensations. He exhorts those who are partakers of the rich grace of the Gospel to follow the example of the children of God under the former Covenant; they should bring their bodies—all their powers and attainments—place them on his altar—a real sacrifice, made holy by the receiving Spirit; acceptable, because the ordained gift, and, therefore, well-pleasing unto the Lord. This would be a reasonable service as opposed to a corporeal or outward form of offering, while the similarity of the service would happily illustrate the Christian duty.

---

[16] Isa. liii, 7, 8; Dan. ix, 26.

"In reading Acts ii, 21," says Angus, "we find it said that *'*Whosoever shall call on the name of the Lord shall be saved;' and the question may be asked, What is meant by calling upon the name of the Lord? Matthew tells us that 'not every one that saith, Lord, Lord, shall enter into the kingdom of heaven,' so that the passage is not to be understood in its literal and restricted sense. On referring to Rom. x, 11–14, and 1 Cor. i, 2, we find that this language, which is quoted from the prophet Joel, implied an admission of the Messiahship, of Christ, and reliance on the doctrines which he revealed." The import of the declaration contained in 1 Sam. xiii, 14, and Acts xiii, 22, that David was "a man after God's own heart," is explained by 1 Sam. ii, 35, where it is said, "I will raise me up a faithful priest, that shall do according to *that which is in mine heart*," which shows the meaning to be that David, in his official conduct, would carry out the divine will.

[Marginal note: How to practically use parallel passages.]

In Joel xi, 28, among the attendant blessings upon Messiah's reign, it is promised, "I will pour out my Spirit upon all flesh." Should one desire to know how broad is the application of this promise he may turn to Gen. vi, 12, and read that "all *flesh* had corrupted his way," which clearly shows that the term flesh thus used refers to all mankind; but *flesh* sometimes means tender and teachable, as in Ezek. xi, 19, "I will give you a heart of flesh," is opposed to a heart of stone. Its more common meaning in the New Testament is corrupt and sinful human nature, as in Rom. viii, 5, "for they that are after the flesh do mind the things of the flesh."

It sometimes signifies, as in Gal. vi, 12, iii, 3, outward ceremonies as compared with inward holiness.

In 1 Cor. vii, 1 Paul says, "It is not good for a man to marry;" but in the twenty-sixth verse he explains his seeming contradiction of the divine assertion that "it is not good that the man should be alone," by saying, "It is good for the present distress" that man should not marry. Marriage is an excellent thing, but may be inexpedient in times of severe persecution.

Sometimes the sacred writers use terms with a very different signification. This must not be overlooked in their comparison. Thus in the epistles of Paul the term "works," when it stands by itself, is used to signify the opposite of faith, the performance of legal duties, as the ground of salvation. In James the expression always means the obedience and holiness which flow from faith. In the one case works are inconsistent with [as the ground of] salvation, in the other they are essential to it.[17] *[Terms sometimes differently used.]*

The different writers of the Gospels supplement each other, and the parallel statements of the same events, when correctly collated, add great interest to the recitals, and aid in their mutual interpretation.[18] *[Gospel writers supplement each other.]*

---

[17] Angus.

[18] To show the additional light and interest which the introduction of the parallel passages in the Gospel throw upon the events which they relate, Dean Alford refers to the accounts of the transfiguration. We learn from Luke the very significant truth " that it was *as Jesus prayed* that the fashion of his countenance was altered." So we read that he was *praying* at his baptism (Luke iii, 21) when the Holy Ghost descended on him. So, too, it is noticed in this Gospel *that he continued all night in prayer.* In a peculiar manner St. Luke brings out this remarkable habit of our Lord in his Gospel. But also in

"In Matt. vii, 13," says Dr. Doedes, "it is evident to every one who pays close attention to the expression, 'Enter ye in,' that we must not think of the way as being behind the gate, as if it were written, Go ye *out* at the strait gate, etc. No; we must think of this gate or entrance as being at the end of that way. The way is not mentioned first, because the gate, as entrance, [to heaven,] is the main subject. To those now who do not understand it thus, and, therefore, place the gate at the commencement of the way, Luke, in chapter xiii, 24, 25, renders good service, where the gate is the same as the entrance, and this can only be thought of as at the end of the way." [19]

<small>The strait gate at the end of the way.</small>

The context is to be carefully examined to discover the meaning of the inspired penman in particular passages. Thus, in Rom. vi, 23, the meaning of the word "death" (the wages of sin) is clearly shown from its opposite, "the gift of God is *eternal life*, through Jesus Christ our Lord." In James ii, 14 the faith that cannot save is explained to be the faith that exhausts itself in words, and not in deeds. It is a faith without obedience, such a faith as

<small>Context to be carefully examined.</small>

---

his narrative of the transfiguration, "we learn what it was on which the three glorified ones conversed on the holy mount: *his decease which he should accomplish at Jerusalem.* Thus does the incident of the transfiguration acquire a holy significance in our Lord's history, which we should not otherwise be able to attach to it. He is now passing into the shadow of his Passion, and the blessed glorified ones are permitted to come and solace his human soul with mention of the sufferings he was to undergo, and the glory which should follow. The transfiguration is the gilded edge of that dark cloud into which the Son of God was entering for our sakes."—*How to Study the New Testament,* page 92.

[19] Hermeneutics of the New Testament, page 102.

devils feel, (verse 19;) but it is not such as Abraham experienced, (verse 23.)

In 1 John iii, 9 it is said, "Whosoever is born of God doth not commit sin." But on comparing this expression with other parts of the epistle we find that to commit sin here means "to walk in darkness," i, 6; "not to keep the commandments," ii, 4; "to hate his brother," ii, 9; "to love the world," ii, 15, expressions that bespeak settled habits, habits alien to the spirit of a Christian.[20]

The affecting and beautiful words of the Psalmist in the forty-second psalm might upon the first reading seem to portray the longing desire of the writer to enjoy the presence of his God in the eternal world:

> "As the hart panteth after the water-brooks
> So panteth my soul after thee, O God!

---

[20] Angus. Dean Alford expresses the severest reprehension of the indolent custom of stringing together in proof of Scripture doctrine passages of the Holy Record, and thus giving to them a signification that could not be sustained by an examination of their contexts. "The utmost that seems to be expected," he remarks, "even from the clergy themselves, is to be able to affirm that the *Scripture* says so and so. But *what* Scripture says it? with what intent? how far, in the words quoted, is the context duly had in regard? do they or do they not rightly represent the sense of the original? these things not one *clergyman* in ten seems to take into account, still less those laymen who would be ashamed to quote in the same slovenly manner any of the well-known classical authors. And as to ordinary English readers of the Gospels, it is not too much to say that the way in which they use them seems to proceed on the assumption that there is but one Gospel, not four; that that one has been delivered down to us entire and indisputable in every point, and in one form, and that form the English version as published by King James's translators."—*How to Study the New Testament*. The satisfactory reliance upon the English version is far from being so serious an evil as the quoting of passages out of their connections, and thus forcing them to sustain a doctrine never intended by the inspired Author.

> My soul thirsteth for God, the living God:
> When shall I come and appear before God?
> My tears are my meat day and night,
> While it is said continually, Where is thy God?"

But the fourth verse of the psalm shows that the devout king, deprived of the privileges of the sanctuary by the rebellion of his son Absalom, which had driven him from Jerusalem, wrote these words to express his inward panting for the beloved services of God's earthly courts:

<small>David sighing for God's house.</small>

> "When I remember these things, I pour out my soul in me;
> For I had gone with the multitude,
> I went with them to the house of God,
> With the voice of joy and praise,
> With a multitude that kept holy day."

The one hundred and tenth psalm describes the victorious progress of an illustrious prince greatly honored by God, and exalted to his right hand. The first three verses leave one in doubt whether the poet speaks of David or another and far greater personage, as the sitting at God's right hand may be figurative:

> "Jehovah said unto my Lord,
> Sit thou at my right hand,
> Until I make thine enemies thy footstool.
> Thy powerful scepter Jehovah sends out of Zion:
> Rule in the midst of thy foes."

<small>Messianic Psalms.</small>

But the fourth verse settles the question:

> "Jehovah hath sworn and will not repent:
> Thou art an everlasting priest
> Of the order of Melchisedek."

David was no priest, nor could any Hebrew monarch assume the office without heaven-daring profanity. The strange and (to the Jew) astounding phenomenon of a "priest upon a throne" directs us at once to David's Son and *Lord*. The application of this simple test will enable the plainest Christian to detect the psalms called Messianic at a glance. They all embody in their representations such remarkable incidents and traits of personal character as make it impossible to apply them, without the grossest impropriety, to any but the "Anointed of the Father." [21]

In gathering proof texts to sustain any supposed doctrine of Scripture great care should be taken to examine the context of each quotation to see if the signification which we give the passage is justified by the sense, thus determined, in which it was used by the inspired penmen. Any writer may readily be made to contradict himself, or to make the most extravagant assertions, by taking sentences out of their connection and giving to them a meaning that they may possibly bear, but utterly opposed to the intention of the author. Certainly no doctrine affecting faith and practice should be built up on separate clauses of Scripture. *Care in gathering parallel passages that their sense be correctly determined.* *No doctrine should be built up on separate clauses of Scripture.*

A clergyman of the modern school of theology called "liberal," in preaching upon our Lord's parable of the prodigal son, inquired, after he had passed through and illustrated its touching recitals, "Where does the atonement come in here? We see nothing of it," *Prodigal son and the atonement.* he continued, "as Jesus brings a penitent son to the Father's arms. *He* should know what is required, and he shows that all that is necessary is only that which a living earthly

[21] M'Lelland.

father seeks, the penitent return of the child to the father's house."

But this same Jesus, our Saviour, in his interview with Nicodemus, opens his discourse with the assertion, "Except a man be born again—born of water and of the Spirit—he cannot see the kingdom of God." He then explains to the wondering rabbi that this divine process is to be secured by looking upon the Son of man, who was to be "lifted up" as "Moses lifted up the serpent in the wilderness." Here is where the atonement comes in! but where does the prodigal son come in in *this* discourse?

These Scriptures present different aspects of the one grand and divine plan of redemption, each one teaching a vital truth, and both indispensable to lead a sinner to a reconciled God. The parable presents the paternal love of God, and the welcome with which the penitent sinner is met as he returns, confessing his sins, to a life of obedience and trust. The words of Jesus to the moral Jew exhibit the divine plan by which God can be just, through the interposition of a Redeemer, and still justify the sinner that believes in Jesus, and the indispensable office of the Holy Ghost in renewing the depraved heart.

We need to collect together from the Scriptures all that is said upon a given doctrine before we declare its full intent and relation to the other elements of a divine life. In 1 Cor. xv, 22 we read, as already quoted, "For as in Adam all die, so in Christ shall all be made alive." On these words we sometimes find built up a theory of the moral and legal identity of our race with our first parents; the text affirms, such interpreters say, that all men die in Adam, therefore all once lived and acted in him. Here is a moral and legal unity, they assert; his sin was our sin, his guilt our guilt, his death our death. On the other hand, another class declares that the text teaches that salvation by Christ is as universal as death by Adam. Do not all men die? they ask. Does not the text say death came by Adam? What then, they inquire, as if the theory were proved beyond a cavil, does the apostle mean, but that all are saved in Christ? Sure enough, what does he mean? Read the context, and the answer cannot be mistaken. Paul is presenting the glorious doctrine of the resurrection of the body. In his argument he says, "For since by man came death, by man also came the *resurrection of the dead.*" As by Adam came upon all men the sentence of death, so by the man Christ Jesus came upon all men the gift of resurrection from the dead. The apostle is writing simply upon the subject of the resurrection, and makes no reference either to the universal salvation of sinners or to the federal relation of all men to Adam. He states simply the obvious fact, that all men have died since Adam's sin, and as a consequence of it; but that the loss of life has been more than amply compensated by Christ's giving it back again in the form of a resurrection to the world. As man is not necessarily lost, even though he may die on account of Adam's sin, so he is not necessarily saved, although he may live forever, as a consequence of the interposition of the Lord Jesus Christ.

<small>All dying in Adam and living in Christ.</small>

It must not be forgotten that the strongest meaning that can be placed upon Scripture terms is not always the writer's acceptation of them; but the context and parallel passages must determine this. Such words as perfect, perfection, holiness, sanctification, without sin, must be carefully considered in the light of their connections and of parallel Scriptures. It must be seen at once that all these terms, as predicated of finite and imperfect beings, cannot have an absolute signification. Because the words, as literally rendered, seem to afford strength to any position we have taken, we have no right to impose a sense upon them that never entered into the mind of the sacred writer. The context and parallel passages must be sought to enable us to weigh their meaning. The beautiful sentence in Jer. xxxi, 3, "I have loved thee with an everlasting love, therefore with loving kindness have I drawn thee," is sometimes made to teach the doctrine of eternal decrees, and the certain salvation of the elect; but God here simply assures the tribes of Israel of deliverance and protection on account of the love he bore them in former times, when with an outstretched arm he brought them from the land of Egypt. In the familiar words found in Matt. xxii, 4, "Many are called, but few chosen," which have been so many times quoted as excluding arbitrarily the unelect from the hope of salvation, the context clearly shows that the Saviour only teaches us that, while all are invited to the Gospel feast, few comparatively are *admitted*, simply from neglecting to secure the necessary and available qualifications.

The strongest meaning not always the true one.

Eternal decrees not taught in Jer. xxxi, 3.

Many called, few chosen.

The Church of Rome gives an amusing illustration of the error we are now considering. In their book of canon law in the chapter relating to lay trustees of Church property, they say, "This is prohibited in the law of Moses, who says, 'Thou shalt not plow with an ox and an ass together;' that is, they shall not have laymen as trustees of Church property!" Church of Rome upon plowing with "ox and ass."

"The phrase, 'Blot me out of thy book,' (Exod. xxxii, 32,) has been made a test of Christian character, so that they who could not say they were willing to be eternally damned have been regarded as destitute of that submission which is the evidence of a new birth. But plainly it had no such force as used by Moses. He meant to say: 'Forget me; take no account of me in respect to any thing proposed concerning the future destiny of thy people; pass by me; regard me as not written in thy book;' without any reference to eternal woe." [22] "Blot me out of thy book."

In reference to that most sublime of all revelations made to man, "God manifest in the flesh," no human presentation of the divine mystery can approach in impressiveness, or even in clearness, the utterances of the sacred writers. No argument setting forth the perfect humanity of our Lord and his essential divinity can be so effective as the collated passages of Holy Scripture. The Word of God becomes flesh before our eyes. We see the perfect human being growing in grace and favor with God and man; eating, sleeping, weeping, tempted, praying; and we also stand awed before Him who heals the sick, casts out devils, commands the waves and the winds, and raises the dead. Surely he can be no other than Emmanuel, God with us The Christ of Scripture.

[22] Doble.

These illustrations might be indefinitely multiplied, but they will serve to impress the young interpreter with the importance of a careful comparison of Scripture with Scripture, and of a close examination of the context.

Rule IV.

Every Scripture must be interpreted in harmony with the analogy or rule of faith; and where a passage admits of two possible renderings, that is to be preferred which best agrees with the general teachings of the writer, and is in harmony with all divine revelation.

If the Bible is all inspired of the Holy Ghost its different parts must be in harmony with each other. There will be unity in the revelations made of God, of his plan of salvation, and of man's condition without the Gospel, and under its influence. This is what is meant by the analogy, or general agreement, of faith. This has been more simply stated, to meet the objection that every distinct sect and every individual interpreter has his own standard of faith or belief, in this form: no interpretation is correct which makes a sacred writer contradict himself, or the well-ascertained sentiments of any of the rest.[23] The apostle Paul recognized this important rule when he exhorted the Roman brethren to prophesy or preach "according to the proportion [or analogy] of faith."[24] The expression is identical with "the whole tenor of Scrip-

Inspiration implies unity.

Analogy of faith.

[23] Doble. [24] Romans xii, 6.

ture." One Scripture passage may contain all that God has been pleased to reveal upon a given subject. It certainly is not to be rejected because it stands alone, if there is nothing in its declaration, when clearly apprehended from its context, that opposes the general tenor of revelation. But if the apparent sense of a given passage is directly opposed to other Scriptures, or to the analogy of faith, an interpretation is to be sought for it which, without constraint to the literal rendering, will bring it into unity with the general teaching of the Bible. It is the legitimate office of the learned expositor to consider and weigh and harmonize these apparent discrepancies. *When one passage may sustain a doctrine. If one passage seems to oppose others it must be interpreted in harmony with them.*

In 1 Cor. iii, 15 we read, "If any man's work shall be burned, he shall suffer loss; but he himself shall be saved so as by fire." "The modern doctrine of purgatory, that is, that sin is purged by literal fire, is derived from this text. Not to insist on the meaning of these words as determined by their connection, we bring this modern doctrine of purgatory side by side with the grand system of doctrines concerning which there never has been any dispute; and the conclusion to which we come is, that any such interpretation of the passage must be false, because it goes contrary to the doctrines of the new birth, of justification by faith, the merits of Christ's atonement, the uniform doctrine of the Bible respecting the souls of the departed, and to many facts recorded both in the Old Testament and in the New."[25] *False foundation of Papal doctrine of purgatory.*

[25] Doble.

All those passages in the Scriptures which speak of God as "repenting," or changing his mind, as coming down to observe what is passing upon the earth, etc., are to be interpreted in such a sense as to harmonize with the revealed truth that God is a Spirit, omniscient, unerring, and everywhere present. In these Scriptures he simply speaks after the manner of men, and does what, if men did these things, would be predicable of them. All passages that seem to represent him as material, local, limited in knowledge or in power, are to be interpreted agreeably to the general tenor of Scripture as to his character and attributes.

Passages referring to God after the manner of men.

No undue wrench is given to the sacred writings by such a course. The necessity arises out of the nature of things. It is entirely reasonable and natural that God should reveal himself in this wise. How can he manifest himself to us but by material figures and words that are necessarily limited in their application? But while he manifests his sentiments and his acts in these finite forms he distinctly declares his spiritual nature and his divine power and Godhead, so that an intelligent mind can readily interpret these human representations in accordance with the spiritual nature of God.

Why God is thus spoken of.

We select from Dobie's "Key to the Bible" two illustrations of the other application of the rule, that where two or more meanings can be drawn from the text, that one is to be chosen which best agrees with the general teachings of the Scriptures. In Matt. xvi, 18 we read, "And I say unto thee, that thou

Of two or more meanings the one in harmony with general teachings of the Bible to be chosen.

art Peter, and upon this rock I will build my Church; and the gates of hell shall not prevail against it." There are at least three distinct shades of meaning which these words may reasonably bear. 1. Upon such confessions as this that thou hast made of my Messiahship I will build my Church; or, 2. Upon this truth that I am Messiah I will build my Church; or, 3. By means of thee, Peter, a man of firm and resolute will, will I lay the foundation of the Church as a distinct community in the world. The first two are both consistent with all scriptural doctrines, are perhaps most commonly received by interpreters, and many considerations may be urged in their favor; but the last is in harmony with actual historical facts recorded in Acts ii, 14-36, and in chapter 10 of the same book, where, by Peter's instrumentality, the Church, composed both of Jews and Gentiles, was established as a distinct body in the world. And such an announcement from the lips of our Lord, in the circumstances, was both appropriate and significant. It was just such an announcement as he was wont to make frequently of what the disciples were to endure and accomplish; and we, therefore, prefer this last sense of the passage according to the spirit of the rule. The words of our Lord when recalled by Peter in the times of stern conflict through which he passed, would administer an unspeakable solace to his heart, and to the hearts of all the other disciples. But there is not one syllable in this text to justify the wild, foolish, and wicked pretenses of the Papal Church founded upon it.

Rock on which Christ builds his Church.

In James v, 20 it is written, "He that converteth the

sinner from the error of his way shall save a soul from death, and shall hide a multitude of sins." This text will bear two renderings. 1. The soul saved, and the multitude of sins that are hid, may refer to the person who reclaims his erring brother; or, 2. They may refer to the brother reclaimed. If we adopt the first, the teaching of the apostle would be, that he who reclaimed a brother from backsliding would save thereby his own soul, and hide a multitude of his own sins. But does the apostle mean this? According to the rule we must consider the design of the writer and the general system of revealed truth. Our impression, upon consideration of the writer's object and line of thought—showing the benefit that would accrue to others through devout and fervent prayer—and of the whole tenor of his teachings in his epistle, is, that his language refers to the person who is reclaimed, and that he holds it out as a motive to action in the work of reclaiming him. As respects the harmony of the first view with the analogy of faith there is no doubt it is wholly at variance with it. We are saved by faith in Christ, not by acts of kindness done to erring brethren. Hence we conclude the meaning of the passage is, He who reclaims a fallen brother is the means of saving a backslider's soul, and of hiding his sins. This is consistent with the design of the writer, and with the general harmony of revelation.

<small>Covering a multitude of sins.</small>

As a general remark in reference to what may be called the difficulties or contradictions of Scripture, it may be said that they afford one of the best evidences that there was no collu-

<small>Difficulties of Scripture evidence of their honesty, and no occasion for discouragement.</small>

THE WORD OF GOD OPENED.

sion between the writers to secure absolute harmony; that they never have been so serious as to discourage good men in their grateful task of studying out the means of their reconcilement; that as knowledge has increased these difficulties have disappeared; that no one, or collection of them, has been considered of so serious a moment as to allow the foes of the Bible to rest their objection to Scripture upon it; but every new school of doubters has discarded the objections of others, and presented fresh ones of their own. Some of these difficulties arise out of the statistics of the Old Testament when quoted with apparent variations in the New, out of the comparison of genealogical tables, and out of the relation of the same event by two evangelists in different words, or the omission or introduction of some one feature of an occurrence by one of the Gospel writers. We have already alluded to the difficulties arising from the adjustment of the new developments of natural science with long received opinions in reference to the interpretation of the Bible. As the enemies of the Bible were never more active than at present in attempting to weaken the faith of Christians in their Holy Scriptures, so, by the good providence of God, there was never a period when so many, and such intelligent and learned pens, were interested in responding to these attacks. There has not been a difficulty or an apparent contradiction suggested that has not been examined. Every obstacle has been fairly looked in the face, and the literature of the Church is now rich in the clearest and most satisfactory defenses of the inspiration

Occasion of these difficulties.

Abundant answers to all difficulties.

and essential harmony and purity of its volume of revealed truth.

The precious works of a former age, such as those of Lardner and Horne, have by no means superseded, and can now be profitably consulted in reference to nearly every difficulty arising about or within the Scriptures. But our modern commentators, like Olshausen, Tholuck, Hengstenberg, Stier, Alford, Lange, Ellicott, Barnes, Whedon, and Nast, meet with great spirit, and with most satisfactory results, the latest imputations of error made by false friends or pronounced foes upon the sacred record. It would swell our book to undesirable proportions to introduce the more prominent difficulties of inspiration suggested by such sincere but unbalanced minds as the author of a late work upon the "Human Element in the Inspiration of the Scriptures." Every difficulty, however, has been met, and may be found fully answered in such volumes as "Lee upon Inspiration," and Garbett upon "God's Word Written."

Ancient and modern apologists.

Where answers to objections may be found.

Every young interpreter may safely assure himself that somewhere, not far from his hand, in the literature which the Master has inspired his disciples to place at the disposition of his Church, a convincing response can be found to every charge. It is proper, however, to guard the teachers of others in this respect. Never venture upon the exposition of a scriptural difficulty without being satisfied that you have a clear and pertinent view of the objection or difficulty, and its answer. Nothing is more harmful than to leave upon an ingenuous young mind an

May be assured an answer can readily be found.

unsatisfactory solution to an apparent difficulty *Never give an unsatisfactory answer.* of Scripture. It is better to leave the difficulty unanswered, with the presumption in the mind of the pupil that the trouble arises rather from want of knowledge in yourself than from any intrinsic contradiction in Scripture. Says Alford, dean of Canterbury, in reference to apparent discrepancies between the evangelists, " We are certain that each of the Gospel narratives is, in the highest sense, true; but we are not certain that we can by sight *Dean Alford upon discrepancies in the New Testament.* assure ourselves, in each apparent case of discrepancy, that it is so. I have elsewhere maintained, and I maintain here, that if we could know exactly how any given event related in the Gospels happened, we should at once be able to account for the variations in the narratives, and the separate truth of each would be shown; but not knowing the exact details of any event thus narrated, nor the position of the narrator with respect to it, we cannot undertake to reconcile apparent discrepancies between the evangelists. Our plain duty in making a right use of the Gospels is firmly and fearlessly to recognize these, and to leave them as fearlessly unsolved if no honest solution can be found. A way may be opened by and by in the process of human discovery, and the toil of human thought, or the time for a solution may not come till the day when all things shall be known." [26]

Henry Rogers happily says, in substance, in his "Greyson Letters:" "My second theory of dealing with the apparent discrepancies of the Bible is a very *Henry Rogers upon discrepancies.*

[26] How to Study the New Testament, page 11.

simple one, and not less admissible, namely, to let them alone; to postpone them till further light is thrown upon them; not to *anticipate* the true theory of them; to refrain from pronouncing them either insoluble or otherwise. The *general* evidence for the Bible is such as to justify this delay. We can *afford* to wait. A Christian may say with justice, 'When I can solve these difficulties, I am glad; when I cannot, I am willing to suspend my judgment; they do not, they never can, (whatever be the solution,) shake the substantive credibility of the great facts and main statements of the scriptural documents; adequate evidence against *these* must be an earthquake which shall subvert the very foundations of the faith and leave the whole fabric a wreck, not a flash of critical lightning, which grazes, or splinters, or even dislodges a stone or two in some remote turret or ornamental pinnacle. I can *wait;* I can *afford* to wait; no one hurries me; why should I be so incontinent of my opinion as to pronounce before I am sure that I have all the possible data? Whether the discrepancies are ultimately to be disposed of by supposing something less than indefectible inspiration for every particle of canonical Scripture, or by finding that they yield, *as so many others have already done*, to more accurate recensions of the text, or more severe collation of the Scripture with itself or with profane writers, or unexpected recoveries of fragments of ancient history, I leave for a while; for, either way, the things which must thus be left are but 'dust in the balance;' subtracted or added, they will not appreciably affect the result; and so, whether zealous Stephen really confounded the sepulcher which Jacob bought of the father of Shechem with that which Abraham bought of Ephron the Hittite or not, I shall magnanimously leave to future inquiries, and sleep none the worse for it.'"[27]

Rule V.

The spiritual instruction intended to be imparted by the Holy Ghost should be carefully and earnestly sought in the interpretation of Scripture.

Revelation is a book written in human language, and as a book is to be interpreted according to the well-defined laws of language and grammar; but it is a book, the whole of which is indited for a special purpose, and of which inspiration itself affirms that it is all profitable "for instruction in righteousness." We are no advocates of a fanciful interpretation of the Bible. We do not believe in mystical significations, or in a manifold sense attributed to the sacred writings. We enjoin a strict grammatical rendering of the text, as modified only by the current meaning of the language used by the writers themselves. But after the exact and literal meaning has been discovered, then comes the important inquiry, What is the spiritual lesson that God proposes to teach in this history, poetry, prophecy, ceremony, parable, miracle, and epistle? We do not by any means propose to spiritualize a secular event, to find types in persons not said in Scripture to be typical, but to ask, What lesson by this plain history, or by the sketch of this individual, would

The Bible a book given for a special purpose.

Not a fanciful nor mystical meaning.

What does God teach?

---

[27] The Greyson Letters, page 461.

the Holy Spirit have us learn? Hagenbach, in speaking of the work of Ernesti in introducing a new and literal school of biblical interpretation, remarks that his "ground principle was simply this: to interpret the Bible according to its literal verbal sense, and to let the volume suffer neither at the hands of any assumed authority of the Church, nor of the feelings and wishes of individuals as to what they might choose to believe, nor of sportive and allegorizing fancy such as the mystics used to indulge in, nor of any philosophical system. He adopted in this the main principle of Hugo Grotius, who in the seventeenth century had similarly intrenched himself. Ernesti was a philologist. He had employed the same principles in the interpretation of the writers of Greece and Rome which he employed later in the interpretation of the Bible; and he was right in this. The reformers had aimed to do the same thing. But he overlooked too much, perhaps, this fact—that in order to apprehend the *religious* truths of the Scriptures there is needed, not only a knowledge of their verbal and historical characteristics, but a spiritual appropriation of their truths, so that one can enter *livingly* into the very heart of the Bible. Who would deny that, in order to understand an epistle of Paul, there must be a very different manner of approaching and viewing it than would be needed with the letters of Cicero, since the whole circle of ideas is different in the two? Religious writings can only be truly apprehended by a penetrating spirit, which can strike through the whole web of grammar and logic to the fundamental truth." [26]

[26] German Rationalism, Clark's edition, page 76.

THE WORD OF GOD OPENED. 165

Westcott happily remarks: "When the interpreter of Scripture has availed himself of every help which historical criticism can furnish for the elucidation of the text—when, by the exact investigation of every word, the most diligent attention to every variation of tense, and even of order, the clearest recollections of every phrase, he has obtained a sense of the whole, perfect in its finer shades and local coloring, no less than in its general outline and effect— his work is as yet only half done. The literal sense is but the source from which the spiritual sense is to be derived; but exactly in proportion as a clear view is gained of all that is special in the immediate object and position of each writer, it will be found that the simple record appears to be instinct with divine life, for the external circumstances and mental characteristics of the writer are not mere accidents; but inasmuch as they influence his apprehension and expression of the truth, they become a part of his divine message, and the typical specialty which springs from this is the condition at once of the usefulness and of the universality of Scripture. The existence of an abiding spiritual sense underlying the literal text of the Old Testament is sufficiently attested by the quotations in the New. Unless it be recognized, many of the interpretations of the evangelists and apostles must appear forced and arbitrary; but if we assume that it exists, their usage appears to furnish an adequate clew to the investigation of its most intricate mazes."[29]

Westcott upon spiritual interpretation.

Horne remarks in his "Introduction," that the errors into which some have fallen in discovering fanciful rather than

---

[29] Introduction to the Study of the Gospels.

spiritual revelations in the Scriptures is not a sufficient reason for rejecting a wholesome principle. It should not be cast away because it has been abused, "since human error can never invalidate the truth of God." "The literal sense," he goes on to say, "it has been well observed, is, undoubtedly, first in point of *nature*, as well as in order of signification; and consequently, when investigating the meaning of any passage, this must be ascertained before we proceed to search out its spiritual import; but the true and genuine, or spiritual, sense excels the literal *in dignity*, the latter being only the medium of conveying the former, which is more evidently designed by the Holy Spirit. For instance, in Num. xxi, 8, 9, compared with John iii, 14, the brazen serpent is said to have been lifted up in order to signify the lifting up of Jesus Christ, the Saviour of the world; and, consequently, that the type might serve to designate the antitype."

[marginal note: Horne on the spiritual import of Scripture.]

We have fully illustrated this rule in the previous chapter, when speaking of the requisition which the discovery of the spiritual lessons of Holy Scripture makes upon the biblical student for careful study.

CHAPTER VII.

INTERPRETATION OF PARABLE, POETRY, AND PROPHECY.

PARABLE.

SOME of the most interesting and instructive portions of the Gospels are embodied in the parables. It has been noticed that, while our Lord from the commencement of his public ministry was accustomed to speak in figurative language, as when he points to the lilies of the field, the fowls of the air, the new cloth upon an old garment, new wine in old bottles, yet his discourses in parables were confined to the last year of his life. The parable has ever been a favorite channel among Eastern people, and especially among Jewish teachers, for the conveyance of truth. But the parables of Jesus are distinguished from all others in their great simplicity, in their wonderful truth to nature, and in the significant spiritual lessons which they teach. *(The parable. Principal parables uttered during the last year of Christ's life.)*

Our Saviour may have adopted the parable to show the harmony between the laws of nature and the doctrines of the Gospel, thus presenting an indirect evidence that they both came from the same Author. Thus the sower of natural and spiritual seed labors under nearly the same general laws of success. *(Reasons for using parables.)*

Tholuck remarks "that the Author of the spiritual kingdom is also the Author of the natural kingdom, and both kingdoms develop themselves after the same laws. For this reason, the similitudes which the Redeemer drew from the kingdom of nature are not *mere* similitudes which serve the purpose of illustration, but are internal analogies, and nature is a witness for the kingdom of God. Hence was it long since announced as a principle, that 'whatever exists in the earthly is found also in the heavenly kingdom.' Were it not so, those similitudes would not possess that power of conviction which they carry to every unsophisticated mind."[1]

<small>Tholuck on the unity of the kingdoms of nature and grace.</small>

By connecting religious truth with natural objects, our Lord would aid his hearers in holding his discourses in their memories. Every lily and bird and merchantman of goodly pearls, every marriage feast, every returning season of seed-sowing, would afresh remind his disciples of the words of Him "who spake as never man spake." But his parables served to illustrate and impress upon the minds of his disciples the truths that he presented. They were blinded by prejudices resulting from their education and Jewish expectations in reference to the character of the Messiah's kingdom, and slow to believe and receive the spiritual nature of Christ's government. "By teaching in parables, and presenting the concerns of his kingdom under the image of familiar objects and earthly relations, he laid the groundwork of a most comprehensive and varied instruction. Many aspects of the kingdom were thus unfolded to them in a form they could easily grasp and distinctly comprehend, though for the time

<small>Aid his hearers to remember his words.</small>

<small>Illustrated and impressed the truth.</small>

---

[1] Tholuck on John xv.

all remained, like the symbols of the Old Testament worship, very much as a dark and unintelligible cipher to their view. That cipher, however, became lighted up with meaning when the personal work of Christ was finished, and the Spirit descended with power to make application of its blessings, and the minds of the disciples were enabled to grasp the higher as well as lower scheme of doctrine exhibited in the representation. Through the earthly form they could now descry the spiritual."[2]

There is one reason which Jesus himself gives for teaching, in the latter part of his ministry, almost entirely in parables: that it was in some sense a rebuke and judgment on his hearers for not receiving the truth when presented in a simple and direct form. At the close of the parable of the sower he answers the question of the disciples, why he thus spoke in parables, by saying, "Unto you it is given to know the mysteries of the kingdom of heaven; but to them it is not given: for whosoever hath, *The parable used to vail truth because it had been neglected.* to him shall be given, and he shall have more abundance; but whosoever hath not, from him shall be taken away even that he hath. Therefore speak I to them in parables: because they seeing, see not; hearing, they hear not; neither understand." "The import of the statement is," says Fairbairn, " that the disciples, having to a certain extent used the privilege they possessed, having improved the talents committed to them, were to be intrusted with more; while the body of the people, having failed to make a similar use of *their* opportunities—remaining destitute of divine knowledge, not-

[2] Fairbairn's Hermeneutics.

withstanding all that had been taught them—were to have their means of knowing abridged, were to be placed under a more indirect and vailed method of instruction. This mode of dealing was in perfect accordance with the whole nature and tendency of the work of Christ in its relation to the hearts of men, which always carried along with it two ends, the one displaying the severity, and the other the goodness of God. From the first he was 'set for the fall,' as well as 'the rising again,' of many in Israel—for the enlightenment and salvation first, but if that failed, then for the growing hardness and aggravated guilt of the people."[3]

<small>This is analogous to all Christ's work.</small>

Mr. Gladstone, the Christian statesman and scholar, remarks in his criticism upon that original and very suggestive

---

[3] Fairbairn. "And now comes," says Dean Alford, in his interesting volume entitled "How to Study the New Testament," "a great and mighty change in our Lord's teaching to the people, recorded for us by St. Matthew alone. He had spoken plainly to them in the sermon on the Mount, and doubtless in many other discourses as he went up and down Galilee. But they had rejected his teaching, plain as it was. From time to time, therefore, he withdrew his plain speaking, and had recourse to a new and hidden method of teaching. The *parable* was a lesson which might be heard and not heard; heard alike outwardly by all, and yet differently by each, according to his capacity for apprehending spiritual truth. Henceforth the Lord teaches in parables, explaining all in private to his disciples. And of these parables we have the richest collection in the thirteenth chapter of this Gospel, (Matthew.) There the whole idea and progress and destiny of the kingdom of heaven are unfolded. Its beginnings among men, in the parable of the sower; its counterfeits, and their treatment by us and by God, in that of the tares; its vast outward extent, from the smallest beginnings, in that of the mustard seed; its inward purifying and transforming power, in that of the leaven; the two ways in which men find it, one by chance in a field which he gives up all he has to buy, another by search, also giving up all to acquire it when found; and then, finally, the ultimate destiny of the good and bad in it, in the parable of the draw-net."—*How to Study the New Testament*, page 62.

volume lately published in England by an anonymous author and entitled "Ecce Homo:" "There is another characteristic of the parables. In all of the greater ones which present their subject in detail, Christ himself, when they are interpreted, fills a much higher place than that simply of a teacher divinely accredited. They all shadow forth a dispensation, which, in all its parts, stands related to and dependent on a central figure; and that central figure is in every case but two our Saviour himself. He is the sower of the seed, the owner of the vineyard, the householder, in whose field of wheat the enemy intermixed the tares; the lord of the unforgiving servant; the nobleman who went into a far country, and gave out the talents and said, 'Occupy till I come;' lastly, the bridegroom among the virgins, wise and foolish. In every one of these our Saviour appears in the attitude of kingship. He rules, directs, and furnishes all. He punishes and rewards. Every one of these, when the sense is fully apprehended, repeats, as it were, or anticipates the procession of the day of Palms, and asserts his title to dominion. They must be considered, surely, as very nearly akin, if they are not more than nearly akin, to declarations of his deity. Two others there are which have not yet been mentioned. One is the parable of the householder, who planted a vineyard and went into a far country, and sent his servants to receive his share of the produce. In this parable our Lord is not the master, but the master's heir, the person whose the vineyard is to be, and who being sent to perform the office in which other messengers had failed, is put to death by the cruel and contumacious

Christ holds the supreme place in the parables.

tenants.[4] But this parable, if it sets forth something less than his kingship, also sets forth much more, and embodies the great mystery of his death by wicked hands. There is, also, the parable of a certain king which made a marriage for his son;[5] a relation which involves far more than had commonly been expressed in his direct teaching among the people. Upon the whole, then, the proposition will stand good, that these parables differ from, and are in advance of, the general instruction respecting the person of the Redeemer in the first three Gospels, and place him in a rank wholly above that of a mere teacher, however true and holy. They set forth that difference from previous prophets and agents of the Almighty, which has been noticed by the apostle in his Epistle to the Hebrews, where he says that 'Moses verily was faithful in all his house as a servant; but Christ as a son, over his own house.'"[6]

<small>First rule: Must fully understand the parable in all its parts.</small> In interpreting a parable it is necessary in the first place *to thoroughly understand it—to have a correct apprehension of the force of its different symbols.* If it relates to a feast, the Jewish custom as to invitations, seats, garments, hours, must be distinctly in the mind. If it relates to natural history, a clear idea must be obtained of the nature of the tree or fruit or grain. For <small>Parable of the wheat and the tares.</small> illustration, in the parable of the wheat and the tares, great interest was added to it in a discourse by Dr. Thomson (son of the author of the "Land and the Book," who was himself born in Palestine, and often laid

---

[4] Matthew xxi.   [5] Matthew xxii.
[6] "Ecce Homo," by the Right Hon. W. E. Gladstone, page 82.

when an infant in the "manger" of a caravansera, or inn) by his explanation of the nature of the "tares" referred to. They are a species of spurious and poisonous wheat, looking at first very much like the true grain in its early growth, and hardly to be distinguished from it as the crop is growing; but its heads never fill out. While the true wheat, its kernels filling out, becomes heavy in its head, and bends upon the stalk, these false tares, with their light tops, stand impudently erect, and readily expose themselves in the harvest to the searching eye and gathering hand of the reaper.

We must next discover from the context, if possible, or from the general scope of the parable, the exact idea that the Saviour intended to illustrate or enforce. There is in every one of them a leading theme. Ordinarily the Saviour states, either before or after he relates them, the object of their utterance. This, above all, is to be seized upon and made to be the key to unlock the vailed meaning of the story. Lisco, in his Commentary, says, "This is the center and kernel of the parable, and till it has been discovered and accurately determined we need not occupy ourselves with the individual parts, since these can only be seen in their true light when contemplated from the proper center. We may compare the whole parabolical representation to a circle, the center of which is the divine truth or doctrine, and the radii are the several figurative traits in the narrative. So long as we do not stand in the center, neither does the circle appear in an entirely round form, nor do the radii seem in their proper order, as all tending to the center, and in beautiful uniformity: this *is*

> Second rule: Learn from context the lesson which the Saviour proposed to teach.

> Lisco upon the kernel of the parable.

secured when the eye surveys every thing from the center: so it is precisely in the parable. If we have brought clearly and distinctly out its central point, its principal idea, then also the relative position and right meaning of its several parts become manifest, and we shall only dwell upon these in so far as the main theme can thereby be rendered more distinct."

Thus the affecting and marvelously appropriate and beautiful parables in the fifteenth chapter of St. Luke were called forth by the taunt of the Pharisees that Christ received sinners, and ate with them. They unfold, under a variety, but closely-related series, of illustrations, the reason for the course he had taken, which had called out the taunts of his unfriendly observers. And he shows that upon the most obvious principles of human nature, which even his foes must recognize, the merciful love and interest of God in behalf of the lost which he had manifested in his course toward the morally abandoned were justified.

<small>Main lesson of parables in 15th chapter of St. Luke.</small>

That most solemn parable of the rich fool, recorded in the twelfth chapter of Luke, was called out by the impertinent interruption of one of his hearers, who, having become convinced of the divine authority of the speaker, lost all further interest in his subject, and simply desired to avail himself of his august decision in the division of his earthly inheritance with his brother. In view of this, how pertinent and how impressive was the Saviour's parable, prefaced by the words, "Take heed and beware of covetousness: for a man's life consisteth not in the abundance of the things that he possesseth;" and closing with,

<small>Parable of the rich fool.</small>

"Thou fool, this night thy soul shall be required of thee: then whose shall those things be which thou hast provided?"

In the instance of the parable in the twentieth of Matthew, on account of the unfortunate interruption of the Saviour's remark by the opening of a new chapter, there is at first some difficulty in apprehending the connection and application of the illustration of the householder and his laborers employed at different hours, especially of the summing up: "So the last shall be first, and the first last: for many be called, but few chosen." By looking back into the close of the preceding chapter we find that Peter, noticing how much emphasis Christ, in his interview with the moral and amiable young ruler, had placed upon the giving up of all his property, with characteristic impulsiveness asks what reward should be their's who had already made this surrender? The Saviour shows him that no sacrifice for his cause would go unrewarded in the heavenly kingdom; but something more was required—service must be rendered with a proper spirit, be persevered in to the end, and the rewards of heaven must be submissively left in the Master's hand. Those whose abilities and opportunities would seem to place them first will some of them be found to be last; and those whose humble gifts and late call into the work might seem to throw them into the shade, may be found to be the first through faithful perseverance for many are called to Christian labor, but few enter upon it with the right spirit, and persevere unto the end.

The householder and his laborers.

Thus it may be seen that each parable has its specific lesson, which it is vital for its comprehension to discover

Individual traits may sometimes be safely selected and made
the basis of discourse if care is taken to show
the connection in which they stand with regard
to the unity of the entire representation.

<small>Individual traits may be carefully used.</small>

This thought naturally introduces the final remark, *that great care should be taken not to interpret separately, and out of their relation to the story of the parable, the different incidents embodied in it.* The great danger in expounding parables is in *overdoing* the thing. Every sentence of the story is made to have as important a function to perform as the whole parable itself.[7]

<small>Third rule: The different parts must not be interpreted out of their connections.</small>

Dr. Fairbairn remarks in reference to two parables which our Lord himself interprets: From them we see "that every specific feature in the earthly type has its correspondence in the higher line of things it represents. Nothing, on the one hand, appears merely for ornament; while, on the other, nothing is wire-drawn, or made to wear a meaning that seems too much for it."

<small>The character of our Lord's interpretation of parables.</small>

Such an interpretation is not to be justified as the one that finds in the fact that "five virgins were wise, and five foolish," that just one half of the number of nominal Christians are true disciples, and the

<small>Illustrations of false inferences.</small>

---

[7] An illustration of this may be found in the peculiar commentary just issued by Rev. W. H. Van Doren upon the Gospel of St. Luke, entitled "A Suggestive Commentary." The touching parables of the fifteenth chapter are fairly over laid and well-nigh deprived of force and beauty by the almost innumerable "suggestions" made upon the different clauses in them. The concrete and touching pathos of the story is lost in the cunning ingenuity disclosed in evolving nice shades of meaning out of the most natural and ordinary expressions. Such commentaries have perhaps a "mission," but they need wise men to be benefited and not abused by them.

other half self-deceived or fallen from grace. Neither may one infer from the parable of the sower that exactly one quarter of those that hear fail to receive the benefit they ought from the preaching of the word.

Even Trench, whose work upon the parables is above commendation, errs at times in laying too much stress upon the subordinate sentences of the parable, and sometimes in seeking a fanciful representation of a plain story. "Thus he makes the parable of the good Samaritan teach the mission and example of Christ. The traveler is 'human nature, or Adam, the head of the race,' who leaves the heavenly city and falls into the power of Satan, and is all but killed. Christ now finds him and restores him. The wine is the blood which Christ shed, and the oil is the anointing of the Holy Spirit. The binding up is the sacraments of the Church. This is a link of 'the chains,' (traditionary interpretation,) for he quotes largely from the early fathers, and is carried away on the flowery stream of their rhetoric with great pleasure." Dobie, in his "Key to the Bible," from whence the preceding remark upon Trench is quoted, adds, "It is no small consolation to reflect that the great mass of plain people, who receive the Bible as the word of God, find but little difficulty in comprehending the precise point aimed at in these Scriptures." *Trench's fanciful interpretation of the parable of the good Samaritan.* *Little difficulty in understanding the simple meaning of a parable.*

POETRY.

A very considerable portion of the Bible, especially of the Old Testament, is given to us in the form of poetry.

This form of revealing truth has added to its attraction in all ages, and rendered it especially adapted to be held in the memory, and to become an abiding comfort when the pious man finds himself deprived of the written text.

Poetry of the Bible.

Sir Patrick Hume, when, hid in a sepulchral vault, "he had no light to read by, having committed to memory Buchanan's Version of the Psalms, beguiled the weary hours of his confinement by repeating them to himself, and to his dying day he could repeat every one without missing a word, and said they had been the comfort of his life by night and day on all occasions."* Probably no portion of the Scriptures has been so constantly quoted, or afforded so much consolation to the devout of all ages and countries, as the poetry of the Bible. The Psalms were read and sung by the Jews in their services from David's time, and they have been read and sung by Christians with as much pleasure and profit down to our day. "Augustine," says Dean Stanley, "was consoled on his conversion and on his death-bed by the Psalms. By the Psalms Chrysostom, Athanasius, Savonarola, were cheered in persecution. With the words of a psalm Polycarp, Columba, Hildebrand, Bernard, Francis of Assisi, Huss, Jerome of Prague, Columbus, Henry V., Edward VI., Ximenes, Xavier, Melanchthon, Jewel, breathed their last. So dear to Wallace in his wanderings was his Psalter that during his execution he had it hung before him, and his eyes remained fixed upon it as the one consolation of his dying

Sir Patrick Hume.

Psalms sung in all times and by great variety of persons.

---

* Life of Sir P. Hume, as quoted by Stanley, page 167, second series.

hours. The sixty-eighth psalm cheered Cromwell's soldiers to victory at Dunbar. Locke, in his last days, bade his friend to read the Psalms aloud, and it was while in wrapt attention to their words that the stroke of death fell upon him. Lord Burleigh selected them out of the whole Bible as his special delight. They were the frame-work of the devotion and of the war-cries of Luther; they were the last words that fell on the ear of his imperial enemy, Charles V."[9]

The usual license allowed in the interpretation of all poetry must be given to the sweet singers of Israel: their rich and figurative language is never to be bent to the severe canons of a grammatical interpretation such as might be applied to the history and to the epistles of the Bible. The ordinary figures of rhetoric, which are to be read in accordance with laws peculiar to themselves and which are found in all our higher grammars, are to be recognized in the interpretation of poetic Scriptures. Here many fall into error in attempting to fasten a doctrinal statement upon the highly-figurative language of these poems. Dobie selects a few passages frequently used as proof-texts to show the habit of many religious writers in this respect:

To be interpreted according to the laws of rhetoric.

Not to fasten a doctrinal statement upon figurative language.

> The wicked are estranged from the womb:
> They go astray as soon as born, speaking lies.
> Their poison is like the poison of a serpent:
> They are like the deaf adder that stoppeth her ear;
> Which will not hearken to the voice of charmers,
> Charming never so wisely.—PSALM lviii, 3–5.

> Thou art he that took me out of the womb:
> Thou didst make me hope on my mother's breasts.—PSALM xxii, 9.

---

[9] History of the Jewish Church, second series.

> Behold, I was shapen in iniquity,
> And in sin did my mother conceive me.
> Purge me with hyssop, and I shall be clean;
> Wash me, and I shall be whiter than snow.—PSALM li, 5, 7.

For from my youth, he was brought up with me,
As with a father;
And I have guided the widow from my mother's womb.—JOB xxxi, 19

> And dost thou open thine eyes upon such a one,
> And bringest me into judgment with thee?
> Who can bring a clean thing out of an unclean?
> Not one.—JOB xiv, 3, 4.

> What is man, that he should be clean?
> And he born of woman, that he should be righteous?—JOB xv, 14.

> I have said to corruption, Thou art my father:
> To the worm, Thou art my mother, and my sister.—JOB xvii, 14.

> They are all gone out of the way;
> They are together become unprofitable;
> There is none that doeth good, no not one.
> Their throat is an open sepulchre;
> With their tongues they have used deceit;
> The poison of asps is under their lips.—ROM. iii, 12, 13.

"These texts," the writer above mentioned remarks, "are made the proof-texts respecting man's character, without any allowance for the nature of the composition, or of the subject-matter of which they treat. But the most illiterate person must see that language such as the above is not the language of sober statement, but of highly-wrought poetic emotion, and for that reason it requires very cautious interpretation." To show still further the error of such a course, he quotes the following passages from the Psalms and Prophets, in which the impossibility of a literal rendering is at once seen:

> Moab is my washpot;
> Over Edom will I cast my shoe:
> Philistia, triumph thou because of me.—PSA. lx, 8.

> But I am a worm, and no man;
> A reproach of men, and despised of the people.—Psa. xxii, 6.

> God came down from Teman,
> And the Holy One from Paran;
> And his brightness was as the light.
> He had horns coming out of his head;
> And there was the hiding of his power.
> Before him went the pestilence,
> And burning coals went forth at his feet.
> He stood and measured the earth;
> He beheld and drove asunder the nations;
> And the everlasting mountains were scattered,
> The perpetual hills did bow;
> His ways are everlasting.—Hab. iii, 3–6.

"Let the naked letter be insisted on in such passages— and why not if in the other?—and what absurdity would be the result? We do not say that poetry of necessity exaggerates even doctrinal statements. The inspired poetry of the Bible contains much doctrine, clearly and fairly stated in the best and most impressive forms. But due allowance must be made for the intensity of poetry when describing the character of man and the ways and attributes of God." *[margin: Effect of literal interpretation of such verses.]*

Dr. Hibbard remarks, in his excellent work upon the Psalms, that the interpretation of the poetry of the Bible is less dependent on verbal criticism than on sympathy with the feelings of the author and a knowledge of his circumstances. "You must place yourself in his condition, adopt his sentiments, and be floated onward with the current of his feelings, soothed by his consolations, or agitated by the storm of his emotions. Your attention is less directed to words than to things. The *[margin: To be interpreted in sympathy with the feelings of the psalmist.]*

meaning of the author is to be determined less by an appea to the niceties of philology than by the general scope."

The poetry of the Bible has been divided into the poetry of the affections and the poetry of the imagination. Of the former we have the Psalms, the Song of Solomon, and the Lamentations of Jeremiah, with detached passages here and there from the prophets. The poetry of the imagination is to be found in the book of Job, but especially in the prophetical writings. "They may be regarded as inspired epics, whose theme is the advent and triumph of a great Deliverer, whose glories, one after another, burst upon the eye of the prophet through the haze which envelopes the future." [10]

Two forms of poetry, of imagination and of the affections.

In the Psalms every human affection finds an inspired expression, and they should be interpreted in view of this their main characteristic. "As every hue of the setting sun is reflected in the mirror of a glassy lake, so in the Psalms is reflected every phase of spiritual feeling, from the deepest humiliation under a sense of sin to the most triumphant rejoicing in the conquest of sin and death by a crucified and risen Messiah. Hope, fear, trust, sorrow, love of God, and hatred of evil, the plaintive mourning of the dove, the roar of inner disquietude, the voice of joy and praise, alternate in these holy songs, and furnish expressions and stimulants for every mood of mind." [11]

Interpreted in view of main characteristic.

The most important external aid for the right understanding of the Psalms is a knowledge of the circumstances under which they were com-

A knowledge of the circumstances of their composition valuable.

[10] Goulburn. [11] Ibid

posed. What an additional interest it gives to the noble "Song of Moses" commencing, "I will sing unto the Lord, for he hath triumphed gloriously," to recollect that it was sung upon the banks of the Red Sea after Israel had passed through it upon dry land, and the hosts of the Egyptians were buried in the returning waves. Dr. Townsend has performed a fine service in his excellent Arrangement of the Bible (a work that ought to be in the hands of every interpreter of the Bible) in introducing the Psalms into the historical Scriptures at the period they are supposed to have been written. The events in the history of the Jewish nation form an admirable "setting," in which these songs of praise, or "songs in the night," appear in their best light. Dr. Hibbard, in his work upon the Psalms, has, with great assiduity, arranged the psalms in the order of their chronology, and preceded them with appropriate references to contemporaneous events. Dr. Townsend's Arrangement of Bible.

Stanley, in his account of the reign of David, introduces with happy effect the psalms that marked the different eras in the life and experience of the king. We can only select, from pages of great interest, the account of the bringing of the ark of God into Jerusalem. The event is related simply in 2 Sam. vi, 2, 18: Ark brought into Jerusalem as illustrated by Stanley.
"David arose, and went with all the people that were with him from Baale of Judah, to bring up from thence the ark of God, whose name is called by the name of the Lord of hosts that dwelleth between the cherubim;" and "he blessed the people in the name of the Lord of hosts." "The psalms which directly and indirectly spring out of th[is]

event'[12] reveal a deeper meaning than the mere outward ritual. It was felt to be the turning-point in the history of the nation. Accordingly, as the ark stood beneath the walls of the ancient Jewish fortress, so venerable with unconquered age, the summons goes up from the procession to the dark walls in front: 'Lift up your heads, O ye gates! and be ye lifted up, ye everlasting doors! and the King of glory shall come in.' The ancient everlasting gates of Jebus are called to lift up their heads—their portcullis grates—stiff with the rust of ages. They are to grow and rise with the freshness of youth, that their height may be worthy to receive the new King of glory. That glory, which fled when the ark was taken, and when the dying mother exclaimed over her new-born son, 'Ichabod!'[13] was now returning. From the lofty towers the warders cry, 'Who is this King of glory?' The old heathen gates will not at once recognize this new-comer. The answer comes back, as if to prove by the victories of David the right of the name to Him who now comes to his own again, 'Jehovah, the Lord, the mighty One, Jehovah, mighty in battle!' and again by this proud title admission is claimed: 'Lift up your heads, O ye gates! and be ye lifted up, ye everlasting doors! and the King of glory shall come in.' Once more the guardians of the gates reply, 'Who is the King of glory?' And the answer comes back: 'Jehovah Sabaoth, the Lord of Hosts, he is the King of glory!' This is the solemn inauguration of that great Name by which the divine nature was especially known under the monarchy. It was, indeed, as the sixty-eighth psalm describes it, a

[12] Psalms xv, xxiv, xxix, xxx, lxviii, cxxxii, and cxli.   [13] 1 Sam. iv, 21, 22.

second exodus. David was on that day the founder, not of freedom only, but of empire; not of religion only, but of a Church and commonwealth. But there were revelations of a yet loftier kind even than this new name of the leader of the armies of Israel. The name of the Lord of Hosts, as revealed in the close of the twenty-fourth psalm, was destined itself to fade away into a dark silence when the hosts had ceased to fight and the empire of Israel had fallen to pieces. But in the hopes with which that same psalm is opened, and which pervades the fifteenth and the one hundred and first, the faith of David takes a higher and still wider sweep. As if in answer to the cry from the guardians of the gates, as he remembers the tabernacle which he had raised within the walls of his city to receive the ark after its long wanderings, as he sees its magnificent train mounting up to its sacred tent on the sacred rock, the thought rises within him of those who shall hereafter be the citizens of the capital thus consecrated, and he asks, 'Who shall ascend into the mount of Jehovah? Who shall stand in his holy place? Who shall abide in thy tabernacle? Who shall abide in thy holy tent?' The question is twice asked, the reply is twice given: 'He that hath clean hands and a pure heart; who hath not lifted up his soul unto vanity, nor sworn to deceive his neighbor. He that walketh uprightly, and worketh righteousness, and speaketh the truth from his heart. He that backbiteth not with his tongue, nor doeth evil to his neighbor, nor taketh up a reproach against his neighbor. He that despiseth a vile person, but honoreth them that fear Jehovah. He that sweareth to his own hurt and changeth not. He that put teth not out his money unto usury, nor taketh a reward against the innocent. He that doeth these things shall never fall.'[14] Of these tests for the entrance into David's city and David's Church one only has become obsolete, that of not receiving usury. All the rest remain in force still—nay, it may even be said that the one qualification, repeated in so many forms, of the duty of truth, even in Christian times, has hardly been recognized with equal force as holding the exalted place which David gives it. When at length the day is past, and he finds himself in his own palace, he there lays down for himself the rules by which 'he will walk in his house with a perfect heart.' The one hundred and first psalm was one beloved by the noblest of Russian princes, Vladimir Monomachos; by the gentlest of English reformers, Nicholas Ridley. But it was its first leap into life that has carried it so far into the future. It is full of a stern exclusiveness, of a noble intolerance. But not against theological error, not against uncourtly manners, not against political insubordination, but against the proud heart, the high look, the secret slanderer, the deceitful worker, the teller of lies. These are the outlaws from King David's court, these alone are the rebels and heretics whom he would not suffer to dwell in his house, or tarry in his sight: 'Mine eyes shall be upon the faithful of the land, that they may dwell with me; he that walketh in a perfect way he shall be my servant. I will early destroy all the wicked of the land, that I may cut off all wicked doers from the city of the Lord.'[15] Many have been the holy associations with which

[14] Psalms xv, xxii.   [15] Psalm ci, 6–8.

the name of Jerusalem has been invested in apocalyptic vision and Christian hymns, but they have their first historical ground in the sublime aspirations of its first royal founder."[16]

This most interesting historical illustration of one series of the Psalms, from Stanley's very instructive History of the Jewish Church, shows how much light can be poured upon them, and how much beauty and force added to them, by a careful gathering of the incidents which formed the first occasions of their utterance.

A marked peculiarity of the poetry of the Bible is a law which seems to pervade the whole of it, and is denominated *parallelism*, an understanding of which will afford great aid in the interpretation of the metrical portions of Scripture. By *parallelism* is meant the correspondence which one line, or a part of a verse, bears to another. The first line will commonly contain a distinct idea or proposition. The second will present the same idea, either more direct and literal, or else more obscure and enigmatical, or perhaps with some enlargement. Sometimes the law of contrast will obtain, and the second or parallel line will be the opposite of the idea contained in the first. In either case it will be seen that it becomes, as it is intended to be, explanatory of the other."[17] *[margin: Parallelism of Psalms.]*

Bishop Lowth presents three forms of parallelism. I. The first he styles *synonymous*, and it embraces those lines that correspond one to another by expressing *[margin: First form: synonymous parallelism.]*

[16] History of the Jewish Church, Second Series, pages 95-98.
[17] Hibbard on the Psalms, page 53.

the same sense in different, but equivalent terms; as, for illustration:

> Because I called and ye refused;
> I stretched out my hand and no one regarded;
> But ye have defeated all my counsel,
> And would not incline to my reproof:
> I also will laugh at your calamity;
> I will mock when your fear cometh.—Prov. i, 24-26.

> Seek ye Jehovah while he may be found;
> Call ye upon him while he is near:
> Let the wicked forsake his way,
> And the unrighteous man his thought;
> And let him turn to Jehovah, and he will compassionate him;
> And unto our God, for he aboundeth in forgiveness.[18]—Isa. lv, 6, 7.

In these selections it will be seen that the thought of the first line is repeated with some variations in the second, and that of the third in the fourth, etc. Sometimes the parallel consists of four lines, the last two answering to the first two, and making one verse:

Sometimes consists of four lines.

> Be not moved with indignation against the evil doers;
> Neither be jealous at the workers of iniquity:
> For like the grass they shall soon be cut off;
> And like the green herb they shall wither.—Psa. xxxvii, 1, 2.

> The ox knoweth his owner,
> And the ass the crib of his lord;
> But Israel doth not know;
> My people doth not consider.—Isa. i, 3.

This order is varied so that four lines will be followed by their four corresponding strains, and at other times the third line will respond to the first, and the fourth to the second.

Eight lines.

---

[18] Bishop Lowth's translation.

> As the heavens are high above the earth.
> So high is his goodness over them that fear him;
> As remote as the east is from the west,
> So far hath he removed from us our transgressions.—PSA. ciii, 11, 12.

II. The second kind of parallels he calls *antithetic*. These are the verses in which the two lines oppose each other by a contrast of sentiments, as, *Second form: antithetic.*

> A wise son rejoiceth his father,
> But a foolish son is the grief of his mother.—PROV. x, 1.

Dr. Hibbard remarks that there is no one rule for the interpretation of the Proverbs of Solomon of more importance and universal application than this law of parallelism. *Peculiar to Proverbs.* In many instances this rule of antithetic correspondence is the chief and only safe reliance of the expositor. Illustrations of this are to be found also in the Psalms.

> Some in chariots and some in horses, (do trust;)
> But we make mention of the name of the Lord our God.
> They are brought down and fallen;
> But we are risen and stand upright.—PSA. xx, 7, 8.

III. The third form is styled *synthetic*. It is where the parallelism consists only in a similarity of construction; neither the words nor lines answer to each other, but there is a correspondence and equality between the different propositions, such as when the parts of speech answer to each other, a negative to a negative, and an interrogative to an interrogative. *Third form: synthetic.* Bishop Lowth illustrates this form by the one hundredth and forty-eighth psalm:

> Praise ye Jehovah, ye of the earth!
> Ye sea-monsters, and all deeps
> Fire and hail, snow and vapor;
> Stormy winds executing his command;

> Mountains and all hills;
> Fruit trees and all cedars;
> Wild beasts and all cattle;
> Reptiles and birds of wing;
> Kings of the earth and all peoples;
> Princes and all judges of the earth;
> Youths and all virgins;
> Old men, together with the children;
> Let them praise the name of Jehovah;
> For his name alone is exalted;
> His majesty above earth and heaven.

The book of Job consists chiefly of this form of parallelism.

> With Him is wisdom and might;
> To Him belong counsel and understanding.
> Lo! he pulleth down, and it shall not be built;
> He encloseth a man, and he shall not be set loose.
> Lo! he withholdeth the waters, and they are dried up;
> And he sendeth them forth, and they overturn the earth.
> With him is strength and perfect existence;
> The deceived and the deceiver are his.—JOB xii, 13-16.

It will prove a pleasant and instructive task to arrange the poetical portions of the Bible into metrical verses under these rules. In Townsend's Arrangement the poetical Scriptures are presented in the form of verse, in accordance with the translation in our received version.

We can hardly leave the poetry of the Bible without a passing reference to the "vindictive psalms," as they are called. There are, as it is well known, portions of these Scriptures in which the most terrible vengeance is denounced upon enemies, extending to their wives and children, even down into the coming generations. No Christian man could use them in reference to personal enemies

The vindictive psalms.

without transgressing the plainest teachings of the Bible, and bringing remorse upon his conscience. It is not a sufficient answer to say that these were the expressions of a dark age and a less merciful dispensation, for in the same book, and dropping from the same lips, are to be found the sweetest, tenderest, most forgiving, and charitable sentiments; and all these strains, it must be remembered, are inspired of the Holy Ghost, and are still *profitable*. There can be but one answer: These are not the expressions of personal wrath against personal foes. As in the instance of the awful and sweeping destruction of human life by the children of Israel when they entered upon the possession of Canaan, there can be found no justification but in the divine command. God might have swept away a frightfully-depraved and sinful people by a pestilence, but this would have seemed to Israel as a natural event, and not a retributive judgment; but he committed the work into their hands, with an express statement of the reason for which he visited this utter destruction upon the nations of Canaan; that they, unarmed and weak as they were, and yet easily, by God's help, overthrowing their foes, might never forget the vengeance that he visited upon idolatry and impurity, nor the sure defense of Him who moved the floods aside for their passage across the Jordan, and made them terrible to God's foes and their own. So in these psalms, there is nothing in the sentiments of the religious men of the Old Testament dispensation, or in the prevailing religious expressions of the psalmists themselves, to justify the opinion that they be-

Not enough to say they bear marks of the age in which they were uttered.

Not expressions of personal wrath.

The psalmists themselves did not believe it right to curse personal foes. lieved it right to curse their personal foes. They were the enemies of God and of his kingdom whom they addressed.

"Job considered it a great sin to indulge a revengeful spirit. 'If I rejoiced at the destruction of him that hated me, or lifted up myself when evil found him; neither have I suffered my mouth to sin by wishing a curse to his soul.'[19] The law of Moses expressly commands kindly offices to enemies.[20] Solomon, also, says, 'If thine enemy be hungry, give him bread to eat; and if he be thirsty, give him water to drink; for thou shalt heap coals of fire upon his head, and the Lord shall reward thee.'[21] 'Rejoice not when thine enemy falleth, and let not thine heart be glad when he stumbleth; lest the Lord see it, and it displease him, and he turn away his wrath from him. Say not I will do so to him, as he hath done to me: I will render to the man according to his work.'"[22] The great psalmist especially, as his treatment of King Saul bore witness, was an amiable, forgiving, noble-hearted man.

These vindictive psalms have been the "songs in the *Have been used by the persecuted of all ages.* night" of the martyrs in all generations. They resounded from the secluded mountains and recesses of Sotland, from the secret retreats of the Huguenots of France, from the fastnesses of the mountains of Tyrol and the Apennines, and from Tabor in Bohemia. Huss, Luther, and the long-suffering of every age have chanted these solemn and inspiring strains of triumph

---

[19] Job xxxi, 29, 30. [20] Exod. xxiii, 4, 5.
[21] Prov. xxv, 21, 22. [22] Prov. xxiv, 17, 18, 29: see Hibbard on the Psalms

against, not their own foes, but the enemies of God and of his Church. It is the same fearful language which the "*Lamb* of God," when upon earth, who received sinners and ate with them, who came to seek and to save the lost, who died with a prayer for his murderers upon his lips, used when addressing the proud, incorrigible foes of God. These psalms set forth in divinely-guarded language God's abhorrence of wickedness, and the fearful judgments he will visit upon those who persist in it. *[margin: Christ used such language.]*

In an elaborate article in the "Bibliotheca Sacra," for January, 1862, Professor Park treats the subject of the imprecatory psalms in an exhaustive manner. In the opening of his paper, as it was written during the civil war, he naturally alludes to the passing events filling the thoughts and anxieties of the land, and remarks that there are crises in human life which bring out the hidden uses of such parts of the Bible as seem long ago to have been rendered valueless through the brighter light of a later dispensation. During the war, he says, "the imprecatory psalms have gained a new meaning in the view of men who have been wont to regard them as unchristian. Now the red planet, Mars, which had been unnoticed in our horizon, has reappeared; the lost hymns have been found again. It is a new proof of the inspiration of the Bible, that so many of its forgotten teachings have been commended to our regard by the martial scenes of the day." References to these terrible utterances of holy writ demand that the one who utters them shall feel the tenderest pity for the suffering as well as a right- *[margin: Prof. Park on the imprecatory psalms. The late war an interpreter of these psalms.]*

eous indignation against wrong-doing. Unless our sympathies be aroused for the bleeding Protestants, we revolt from the sonnet of Milton 'on the late massacre in Piedmont:'

> '*Avenge*, O Lord, thy slaughtered saints, whose bones
> Lie scattered on the Alpine mountains cold;
> Ev'n them who kept thy truth so pure of old,
> When all our fathers worshipped stocks and stones.
> *Forget not!*'

Dr. J. J. Stewart Perowne, in his admirable work upon the Psalms, while affirming the impersonal and right-eous indignation expressed in the imprecations found in the Psalms, regards the spirit of them as unjustified in the New Testament dispensation. "Surely," he says, "there is nothing in such an explanation which, in the smallest degree, impugns the divine authority of the earlier Scriptures. In how many respects have the harsher outlines of the legal economy been softened down by the 'mind that was in Jesus Christ.' How much is declared to be antiquated, even though it still stands for our instruction in the volume of the Bible. How clearly our Lord himself teaches us that his spirit and the spirit of Elijah are not the same. Yet surely no prophet of the Old Testament occupies a higher place as an inspired messenger of God than the prophet Elijah. Our Lord does not condemn the prophet for his righteous zeal; he does forbid the manifestation of a like zeal on the part of his disciples. As in the Sermon on the Mount he substitutes the moral principle for the legal enactment, so here he substitutes the spirit of gentleness, meekness, endurance of wrong, for the spirit of fiery though righteous indignation."

[sidenote: Perowne's view of these psalms.]

"An *insulated* imprecation repels men who will be reconciled to it when they *enter into* such reasons for it as are intimated in Psa. ix, 13–20; x, 2; liv, 3."[22]

The books of Proverbs and Ecclesiastes form the great divine repositories of inspired moral maxims. The histories and biographies of the Bible, as we have said in another place, do not give expression to the divine abhorrence of wrong-doing in the instance of those whose acts are recorded; but in these books, in the most striking and pungent manner, and in a form to cling to the memory, as well as to impress the imagination, the judgment of God against every form of deceit and impurity is given. They are rendered even more impressive as being the results of human experience; coming from the lips of the wisest, richest, most powerful, and most tempted of kings. It is to be feared that in modern days these consummate lessons of wisdom for the guidance and defense, especially of youth, do not receive the attention they should.

<small>Proverbs and Ecclesiastes.</small>

We have already intimated the light that a knowledge of the oriental espousal and marriage customs will shed upon that most incomprehensible, to many, of the books of the Bible, Solomon's Song. Isaac Taylor happily remarks that this song of pure conjugal love carries us back to Eden. In its pure and virgin arbors the king, turning away from the impure atmosphere of a fallen world, finds his subjects and his images. This poem would be entirely true to nature if man only were innocent, and woman always pure and loving. "If," says the well-known author

<small>Solomon's Song.</small>

[22] Bibliotheca Sacra, vol. xix. p. 207.

of the History of Enthusiasm, to whom we have alluded, "a half dozen heedlessly rendered passages of our English version were amended, as easily they might be, then the canticle would well consist throughout with the purest utterances of conjugal fondness. Happy would any people be among whom there was an abounding of that conjugal fondness which might *thus* express itself." It is not as an expression of pure and innocent love merely that it finds its place in the canon, has held it persistently against many efforts to unseat it, and has been found to be a medium of expression among the holiest of the saints of earth, but as the inspired illustration of the deepest and sincerest emotions of their spiritual life. It is to be interpreted in all the simplicity and purity of an early, well assorted, divinely instituted marriage, while under its folds of human love lays embalmed the divine symbol of Christ's relation to his Church and to the individual soul that pants for him. In this use of it "it has served to give animation and intensity, and warrant, too, to the devout meditations of thousands of the most holy, and of the purest minds. Those who have no consciousness of this kind, and whose feelings and notions are all 'of the earth—earthy,' will not fail to find in this book that which will suit them for purposes sometimes of mockery, sometimes of luxury, sometimes of disbelief. Quite unconscious of these perversions, and happily ignorant of them, and unable to suppose them possible, there have been multitudes of unearthly spirits to whom this — the most

Marginalia: A few emendations in text would make it perfect in its expression of holy love. — Prized for its expression of spiritual life. — Isaac Taylor's view of the book.

beautiful of pastorals—has been not indeed a beautiful pastoral, but the choicest of those words of truth which are 'sweeter than honey to the taste,' and 'rather to be chosen than thousands of gold and silver.'"[24]

PROPHECY.

The Bible is full of prophecy fulfilled or unfulfilled. Its histories are the records of the fulfillment of previous prophecies, and the New Testament is the complement of the Old, in which its prophetic types and words are shown to have been fully met in the person of Christ, and the Gospel which he established. *Prophecy.*

It not unfrequently occurs, however, in the New Testament, that an incident recorded in the Old, which in some measure is repeated in the times of Christ, is said to be fulfilled. "Any thing," says Dr. Bloomfield, "may be said to be fulfilled if it admits of being appropriately applied." Thus in the second chapter of Matthew we read, "Then was fulfilled that which was spoken by Jeremy the prophet, saying, In Rama was there a voice heard, lamentation and weeping, and great mourning, Rachel weeping for her children, and would not be comforted because they are not." In the prophetic vision of the weeping seer,[25] the beloved wife of Jacob, the mother of Israel, by a striking figure is represented as rising from her grave and weeping over the slain of her children—slain in the invasions of their country by the foes whom God permitted to scourge them; so in the times of the infant *Illustrative events.* *Weeping of Rachel.*

[24] The Spirit of the Hebrew Poetry, page 239. [25] Jer. xxxi, 15.

Redeemer, when Herod's sword was reeking with the blood of the children of Judea, slain around the very grave of Rachel, near Bethlehem, this sad mother is said to rise and weep again, and the vision of the prophet is once more realized.

The quotation in the fifteenth verse of the same chapter of Matthew is another instance of the same form of fulfillment, or renewed realization: "That it might be fulfilled which was spoken of the Lord by the prophet, Out of Egypt have I called my son." The departure of Israel from Egypt under Moses, of which Hosea speaks,[26] was not a direct prophecy nor type of our Redeemer's brief residence in that country, but a coincident fact, full of profitable and grateful suggestion, and illustrating our Lord's departure from the Holy Land and return to it.

<small>Calling out of Egypt.</small>

Fulfilled prophecy is best interpreted by history. The records of Jewish, Assyrian, Persian, Grecian, Roman, and modern history, and the ruins and desolations of many countries like Palestine and Egypt, and cities like Tyre and Babylon, afford the best means for a correct interpretation of the inspired visions which it pleased God to bestow upon the ancient seers, and which have been signally fulfilled. The prophet himself evidently did not always understand the force of the words or the symbols which he used.[27] The idea of exact time was not in the prophet's mind, for the commencement of Messiah's reign upon earth and the glorious universal triumph of the Gospel are announced in the same passages. It was partly for this reason that the Jewish interpreter, eagerly

<small>History interprets fulfilled prophecy.</small>

<small>Prophet no idea of time.</small>

---

[26] Hosea xii, 13.   [27] 1 Peter i, 10, 11.

seizing upon the triumphs of the promised royal seed of David as connected with the advent of Messiah, overlooked the humiliation and suffering which he must first undergo. *That* manifestation of the Son of David is yet, after nineteen hundred years, an object of faith and not of sight.

It is evident that prophesy is not given in terms so definite as to be readily understood, except as to its general scope. There is not a more definite prophecy than Daniel's as to the time of the coming of the Messiah; yet our Lord, when justifying to his forerunner his claim to the exalted character of Him "that was to come," appealed not to Daniel's symbolical beasts, or to his mysterious figures, but to the miracles of mercy, lying here and there upon the bosom of prophecy, which he was then fulfilling. Christ's own prophecies and those of the book of Revelation are of the same nature. They point out a future with a dark, heavy, crimson foreground, but with a golden and glorious distant horizon. The destruction of Jerusalem, and the final successive subsidence, in connection with much human sorrow and Christian discipline, of other earthly kingdoms, down to the hour of the fall of the last foe and the sublime installation of Christ's universal kingdom, amid the halleluiahs of angels and redeemed men, are set forth in natural and somewhat mysterious symbols in the last discourses of our Lord and the prophecies of John the Evangelist. *Jesus did not appeal to the figures of Daniel.* *Prophecies of the New Testament.*

Prophecy was not intended to be history, but an index or gnomon pointing in the direction of the Divine Providence. It was intended, by the assurance *Prophecy not history.*

it affords when its terms are fulfilled by the occurrence of events, to establish the faith of God's people as to his control of human affairs, as to the inspiration of his word, as to his abundant power to make even the wrath of man praise him, and also to give courage and comfort to the people of God in reference to the future. However discouraging the condition of the Church at any given period, and however arrogant and numerous her foes, the servants of the most high God have a "sure word of prophecy" shining like a bright light upon a dark future, and giving them absolute assurance of the final triumph of Christian truth.

<small>Points to the triumph of Christian truth.</small>

The sad mistakes to which we have heretofore alluded, arising out of a too confident reliance upon a literal rendering of prophetic symbols—the absolute errors into which learned and good men have fallen when apparently resting upon the exact demonstrations of scriptural figures—should teach us the truth of the saying of our Lord, that while his coming will certainly be experienced, with all its attendant circumstances, the specific hour has not been revealed.[28] It seems to have been the intention of the

<small>The hour of Christ's coming not revealed.</small>

---

[28] Matt. xxiv, 36. "But the key," says Dr. Whedon in his supplementary note to his comments upon the twenty-fifth chapter of Matthew, "to the whole mystery (in reference to the time of Christ's second coming) is furnished in 2 Peter iii, 8, where, in regard to this very point, Peter reminds us that 'one day with the Lord is as a thousand years.' (Not that a day in prophecy, as some teach, is an exact symbol of a thousand years, but that time is without human measure in God's mind.) Scoffers in the last days, he tells us, would raise this very objection: 'Where is the promise of his coming?' Peter replies by informing us that the distance of the event is to be measured by the arithmetic of God. One day is as a thousand years, and language that would seem to intimate a *few days* may really embrace a *few thousands* or *myriads* of years. If it be true that both Christ and his apostles have warned us that the time of the second

Holy Spirit that in all ages, even the apostolical, the Church should be looking for and loving the appearing of the Son of God, and purifying herself in the expectation of it. "Only a few years ago," says Dobie, "the year and the day were confidently fixed when the trumpet should sound and the voice of the Son of God be heard calling the world to judgment. It is only as yesterday that the eloquent Irving, with saintly and joyous countenance, was wont to stand for hours together on his balcony, looking toward the east, momentarily expecting to see the glorious white throne, and the retinue of attending angels, and the ever-blessed Redeemer coming in the glory of the Father to judge the living and the dead. And now another prophet has risen up, and by him we are confidently assured from a devout and prayerful study of the prophets that the second coming of Christ and the end of the present system will probably take place in 1865. (The writer refers to the eloquent Dr. Cumming, of London, whose date has now been passed some three years; but, not discouraged, he still fixes it again in the near future.) The data of this and all other similar calculations are found in Dan. xii, 11, compared with Rev. xii, 5; xiii, 18; and xx, 4. But by a cursory inspection of these passages it will be seen that any calculation of the year when this world shall end must be very, if not purely, arbitrary, inasmuch as there is no direct

Irving on the coming of Christ.

Dr. Cumming, likewise.

advent was to them unrevealed and unknown—if they use in abundance terms indicating an indefinite distance—if they themselves furnish the solution of all their expressions intimating its near proximity—all objections to their infallibility in regard to other subjects upon which they speak with professed inspiration are nugatory and captions."

reference to that event in these passages whatever. All that

Bible view of the end. the Bible justifies us in believing respecting the termination of the present world is, that there is a certain grand result to be reached in the history of our race, a general dispersion of the ignorance of men and a triumph over the wickedness that reigns in the earth; and that after an extended period of peace and holiness, very suddenly and unexpectedly the angel of God will summon both the living and the dead to judgment. Then will come the end, the dissolution of the present system in liquid fire, and the final retribution of the last day, dispensed in righteousness by our Lord Jesus Christ." [29] This may, and may

---

[29] Key to the Bible, pages 202, 203. "The Bible," says Bernard, "is one long account of the preparation of the city of God. That is one distinct point of view from which the Bible ought to be regarded, and one from which its contents will appear in clearer light. We are accustomed in the present day to read it too exclusively from the individual point of view, as the record for each man of that will of God and that way of salvation with which he is personally concerned. This it is, but it is more than this. It places before us the restoration not only of the personal, but of the social life; the creation not only of the man of God, but of *the city of God;* and it presents the society or city not as a mere name for the congregation of individuals, but as having a being and life of its own, in which the Lord finds his satisfaction and man his perfection. The 'Jerusalem which is above' is, in relation to the Lord, 'the bride, the Lamb's wife;' (Rev. xxi, 9;) and in relation to man, it is 'the mother of us all.' Gal. iv, 36. In its appearance the revealed course of redemption culminates, and the history of man is closed; and thus the last chapters of the Bible declare the unity of the whole book by completing the design which has been developed in its pages and disclosing the result to which all preceding steps have tended. Take from the Bible the final vision of the heavenly Jerusalem, and what will have been lost? Not merely a single passage, a sublime description, an important revelation, but a conclusion by which all that went before is interpreted and justified. We shall have an unfinished plan, in which human capacities have not found their full realization, or divine preparation their adequate result. But as it is, neither of these deficiencies exists. The great consummation is

not, be the order of events. This millennial reign may come before or after Christ's advent. The former is the widely-received spiritual view of the prophecies, the latter the view of Millenarians, many of whom do not, however, attempt to designate the period when Christ will make his appearance. *Spiritual and literal view.*

But the study of prophecy is profitable, although we may not be able to read it as we would history. It is given, the most of it, in the sublimest strains of poetry ever written, and is to be interpreted according to the rules already laid down for this style of composition. What higher or more spiritual or practical conception of the glory and holiness of Almighty God can be found than that *Prophecy a profitable study.*

---

there, and we are instructed to observe that from the first the desires of men and the preparations of God have been alike directed toward it. At the beginning of the sacred story the father of the faithful comes forth into view, followed by those who are heirs with him of the same promise; and they separate themselves to the life of strangers, because they are 'looking for a city which hath foundations, whose builder and maker is God.' In due time solid pledges of the divine purpose follow. We behold a peculiar people, a divinely-framed polity, a holy city, a house of God. It is a wonderful spectacle this system of earthly types, thus consecrated and glorified by miraculous interventions and inspired panegyrics. Do we look on the fulfillment of patriarchal hopes or on the types of their fulfillment? on the final form of human society or on the figures of the true? The answer was given by prophets and psalmists, and then by the word of the Gospel, finally by the hand of God, which swept the whole system from the earth. It was gone when the words of the text were written, and when the closing scene of the Bible presented the New Jerusalem, not as the restoration, but as the antitype of the old. This vision teaches us that the drama of the world must be finished, and its dispensation closed, that the Lord must have come, the dead have been raised, the judgment have sat, the heaven and earth which are now have passed away, and the new creation have appeared, before the chosen people shall see the city of their habitation."—*Progress of Doctrine in the New Testament*, page 219.

presented by the prophet Isaiah, when in the commencement of his prophetic mission, "In the year that King Uzziah died," he had that sublime vision in the temple.[30] Before his wondering gaze " the vail of the temple was withdrawn and the holy of holies discovered to the prophet's eyes, and he saw the Lord sitting as a king upon his throne actually governing and judging. His train, the symbol of dignity and glory, filled the holy place; while around him hovered the attendant seraphim, spirits of purity, zeal, and love, chanting in alternate choirs the holiness of their Lord; the threshold vibrated with the sound, and the 'white cloud' of the divine Presence, as if descending to mingle itself with the ascending incense of prayer, filled the house. The eternal archetypes of the Hebrew's symbolic worship were revealed to Isaiah; and, as the center of them all, his eyes saw the King, the Lord of Hosts, of whom the actual rulers from David to Uzziah had been but the temporary and subordinate viceroys. In that Presence even the spirits of the fire which consumes all impurities, while none can mix with it, cover their faces and their feet, conscious that they are not pure in God's sight, but justly chargeable with imperfection; and much more does Isaiah shrink from the aspiring thoughts he had hitherto entertained of his fitness to be the preacher of that God to his countrymen—he, a man of unclean lips, sharing the uncleanness of the people among whom he dwells. In utter self-abasement he realizes the exceeding sinfulness of sin, and the utter separation it makes between man and the holy God."[31]

[30] Isaiah vi.   [31] Sir Edward Strachey's Hebrew Politics, page 79.

Prophecy is really a grand epic, with many acts and a variety of scenes, but with a divine unity. Imagination can find in no human work so fine a field for its highest and purest conceptions. Christ is the great central personage in the extended poem, written by different hands, but always preserving the divine unities. His kingdom in all its fortunes, adverse and prosperous, is set forth. His own marvelous history from the manger to the cross, his providential government, and his final universal triumph and coronation in his own New Jerusalem, where his happy followers "need no candle, neither light of the sun, for the Lord God giveth them light," "and there shall be no night there," are presented throughout the long poem, commencing in Eden and ending in the Apocalypse.

Dr. Schaff remarks of the Book of Revelation that it surpasses all the other prophetic writings in harmony, elevation, fullness, unity of view, progress of action, majesty of style, and, above all, in the direct relation of all parts of the picture to the central figure of the crucified and now glorified Christ, who rules the whole history of the world and the Church, and is alpha and omega, the beginning and the end. He goes on to say that "in a succession of visions and mysterious allegories it unfolds before the reader the great epochs of the kingdom of God on earth to the close of its earthly development. Its burden is the comforting truth that the Lord comes, the Lord fights, the Lord conquers and leads his Church through tribulation and persecution to certain victory and eternal glory." He also remarks that the value of the book is quite distinct from any

Dr. Schaff upon the Revelation.

human exposition of its prophecies; that it was not designed to gratify idle curiosity concerning the future, but for a practical, religious end. "Prophecy," he says, "in the nature of the case, remains more or less obscure until it is fulfilled. And as the Old Testament became clear only in the New, so the Revelation of John can be perfectly understood only in the triumphant and glorified Church. Still it has been a book of consolation and hope to the Church militant in every age, especially amid her great persecutions and struggles; and it will remain so till the Lord come again in glory, and the New Jerusalem come down from heaven as a bride adorned for her husband. He who cannot lie assures his people, 'Lo, I come quickly. Amen.' And his people answer with the holy longing of a bride for her spouse, 'Yea; come, Lord Jesus!'" [32]

[32] History of the Christian Church, vol. 1, p. 109.

CHAPTER VIII.

THE BIBLE IN THE WORLD'S LITERATURE.

THE Christian world is presenting an anomalous spectacle at the present hour. There never was a period when her sacred volume, embodying the world's faith and salvation, had so wide a distribution, or was exercising so mighty an influence upon the world's civilization and progress. Nations, both Christian and unchristian, that heretofore have forbidden the introduction of the Bible, have ceased their opposition, and the leaves from the tree of life for the healing of the nations are falling upon every land. In more than two hundred different languages the peoples of the earth are permitted to read the word of God "in their own tongue, in which they were born." By a divine conviction as to its authority and power, which unites nearly all the branches of the visible Church in wonderful harmony of sentiment and charity, the great societies of England and America are enabled to keep their groaning presses constantly in motion in the multiplication of editions of this marvelous book.

<small>Bible never before so widely distributed.</small>

While all this is manifest, at the same moment we behold one of the fiercest, most systematic, and bitter attacks upon the Christian Scriptures in the three leading modern tongues — English, German, and French — carried on with extraordinary vigor, and with

<small>Bitter attack upon it.</small>

some outward manifestations of a limited success. "There is," says an earnest writer in the *British Quarterly Review*, "coming upon the Church a current of doubts deeper far and darker than ever swelled against her before—a current strong in learning, crested with genius, strenuous, yet calm in progress. It seems the last grand trial of the truth of our faith. Against the battlements of Zion a motley throng have gathered themselves together. Socinians, Atheists, doubters, open foes and bewildered friends are in the field, although no trumpet has openly been blown, and no charge publicly sounded. There are the old desperadoes of infidelity—the lost followers of Paine and Voltaire; there is the stolid, scanty, and sleepy troop of the followers of Owen; there follow the Communists of France, a fierce, disorderly crew; the commentators of Germany come, too, with pick-axes in their hands, saying, 'Raze it, raze it to the foundations.' There you see the *garde-mobile*, the vicious and vain youths of Europe. On the outskirts of the fight hangs, cloudy and uncertain, a small but select band, whose wavering surge is surmounted by the dark and lofty crest of Carlyle and Emerson. 'Their swords are a thousand,' their purposes are various. In this, however, all agree—that Christianity and the Bible ought to go down before advancing civilization." The weight of this mighty movement, however, comes from within rather than from without the nominal Church. Unbelief at this hour is baptized, and aims her powerful blows against the very foundations of the Christian faith, in the pretense of laboring in the interests of Christianity herself. These sub-

Foes under the garb of friends.

tle foes, says Tullidge, have skillfully adapted their attacks to the refinement and intelligence of the age, and with a great show of learning and science, and not seldom under the garb of reverence for the Bible and adherence to Christianity, have aimed the most deadly blows against the records of our faith. Colenso is a bishop of the Protestant Episcopal Church, Theodore Parker was an ordained minister over the "Twenty-eighth Congregational Church of Boston;" and Dr. Peabody very truly remarks, that the author of the "Age of Reason," if he had lived at this day, might have published his tracts over the title of Rev. Thomas Paine, and occupied a professedly Christian pulpit. The double object of the present crusade (which is, after all, but one, for the Bible is God's word written, and Christ is the word made flesh) is to secure a religion without a Bible, and a Gospel without a Christ. Rev. Mr. Frothingham says he "reads the Bible as any other book, criticises it, judges it, but expects no superhuman wisdom from it, and will not call it the word of God, or the book in which the words of God are especially written." *Object of attack on both Christ and the word of God.* Another of the same school, in their organ, the "Radical," blasphemously remarks, "It is time to let Jesus rest. Jesus is made a stumbling-block to the generation." "He does not wish to hear any more about him." It is the same condition of things now as in apostolic times: to the unbeliever Christ is still a stumbling-block, and to the infidel foolishness.

It is affirmed with some appearance of truth, by the *Westminster Review*, that the great body of the "mental food of the day — science, history, morals, poetry, fiction, and essay — is prepared by men who have long ceased to believe."

The divine authority of revelation, the authenticity and genuineness of the various books composing it, form the main object of attack. A German writer has aptly remarked: "One period has fought for Christ's sepulcher, another for his body and blood, the present period contends for his word." And this is, indeed, the great question of the hour. The author of Liber Librorum closes his volume with the forcible remark, "The truth or falsehood of the Bible, its worth, or its worthlessness, is the great question of the day. It is not too much to affirm that the life or death of modern society hangs upon the issue."

<small>The era of the contest for the word.</small>

We have not a moment's hesitation or anxiety as to the result. The world has not been redeemed to be thrown away. Too marked a Providence has guarded the Holy Scriptures in darker hours than the present to yield them now to unholy hands. "The gates of hell shall not prevail" against them. "Heaven and earth shall pass away," but Christ's "words shall not pass away." There has not been a generation since these holy writings have assumed the form of a distinct and completed revelation in which they have not been fiercely attacked, but their foes have been shattered like the surges of the sea beating against a mighty reef, while they have remained unmoved as the "Rock of Ages." "The waves of the sea are mighty, and rage terribly; but the Lord who sitteth on high is mightier."

<small>No occasion to be anxious for the result.</small>

THE WORD OF GOD OPENED.   211

It is an encouraging fact, that while the foes of the Bible are united like Herod and Pilate in their enmity toward the word of God, they are hopelessly divided in the weapons they use to accomplish their object. In nothing is the weakness of the argument against the Bible more manifestly seen than in the lack of agreement among its foes. The French school denounces the German, and the English both the others; while different writers in the various nations utterly disagree among themselves, and strenuously affirm the folly of all theories save their own.

But the Bible has gained, as it always must, from these attacks. "They that be with us are more than they that be with them;" and "if God be for us, who can be against us?" If Germany has produced a Strauss, a Bruno, a Bauer, an Eichhorn, a Paulus, and a Schenkel, she has also given for the defense of God's word a Tholuck, a Hengstenberg, a Neander, an Olshausen, a Stier, a Lange, a Ritter, and hundreds of others less prominent, but constantly throwing their sanctified literature as a healthful leaven into the intellectual and religious life of the continent. If Renan has turned the Gospel story into a romance, and made the principal actor a weak enthusiast and deceiver, Guizot and a Pressensé and others have immediately proffered to France more than an effectual antidote. The tracts and essays of too liberal Christians in England, the irreverent writings of Theodore Parker, the sad oracles of the authoress of "Broken Lights," the raw mathematics of Colenso, have awakened into life the most vigorous and brilliant pens of the age: Westcott, Ellicott, Lee, Rogers, Buchanan, Isaac

Bible gained from these attacks.

Taylor, and Bayne; the preachers of the successive Boyle and Bampton University Lectures, Alford, M'Cosh, Fisher, and the unannounced authors of Ecce Deus, Ecce Homo, Liber Librorum, *et id omne genus*, whose names one cannot number. It will be understood, of course, in presenting this list of names, that we do not indorse or accept all the lines of defense chosen by the writers which we have enumerated, particularly in the case of the anonymous authors, but mention them as gallantly accepting the challenge thrown down by the enemies of the Christian Scriptures.

Indeed, one of the most striking evidences of the divine origin and power of the Bible is the prodigious literature which it has gathered around itself. Coming for the most part, as its different books have, from the pens of unlearned men, without the training of the schools, it has gained the most amazing hold upon the human intellect and heart, and set in motion, in all ages, the most powerful and polished minds in explanation, illustration, and defense of its truths and revelations. How true are those expressive words of the apostle Paul, "The word of God is quick and powerful;" that is, it is quickening, life-giving, inspiring! What an immense proportion of the literature of the world would leave its libraries if all growing directly out of the Holy Scriptures should be removed. How has it quickened the human mind in the whole field of the natural sciences and of philosophy! To defend or attack the Scriptures what an interest has been taken in the study of astronomy! What an inspiration the friends and foes of the Bible have felt in the study of geology, from its

[margin note: This prodigious literature an evidence of its divine origin.]

apparent relation to the early chapters of Genesis. The secrets of chemistry have been searched in the hope of producing life without seed, and thus impugning the records of Moses. Every theory of mental philosophy is at once drawn out into line for the defense or overthrow of the doctrines of Scripture. Philology, the origin and antiquity of the race, history and geography, numismatics, in short, the whole circle traversed by human thought and investigation, have been quickened into life by the words of Him of whom it was said, "In him was life; and the life was the light of men."

No book of human authorship could bear up such a literature. The only other volume that may be said to have a literature of its own, which stands at the head of human productions for the universality and power of its influence, only serves to show more significantly the superhuman vitality of the Bible. Who will think for a moment of comparing the influence of Shakspeare with that of the Bible? *Its influence compared with Shakspeare.* But what is the secret of the power of this writer, and whence did he derive it? An English clergyman, Rev. T. R. Eaton, has written a book entitled "Shakspeare and the Bible," in which he seeks to show how much the immortal bard was indebted to the Scriptures for his illustrations, rhythms, and modes of expression. The author affirms that Shakspeare went first to the word and then to the works of God. "In shaping the truths derived from these sources," says an intelligent physician, "he obeyed the instinct implanted by Him who had formed him Shakspeare. Hence his power of inspiring us with sublime affection for that which is properly good, and of chilling us with horror by his fearful delineations of evil. Shakspeare perpetually reminds us of the Bible by an elevation of thought and simplicity of diction which are not to be found elsewhere."[1] Rev. Mr. Eaton points out hundreds of quotations, allusions, and parallelisms in his works, showing Shakspeare's familiarity with Scripture, his fondness for it, and the almost unconscious recurrence of it to his mind.

Few short poems have impressed thoughtful men more than the "Elegy in a Country Church-yard," by Gray, the poet. It has been translated into a number of languages. Dr. Johnson read it with pleasure, and Mr. Webster had his son read it to him upon his death-bed. We are pleased to call to mind the fact that the young and cultivated General Wolfe, while sailing down the St. Lawrence on the eve of his great victory upon the Heights of Abraham, recited the verses of this poem aloud, and said at their close, "Now, gentlemen, I would prefer being the author of that poem to the glory of beating the French to-morrow!" Gray was a fine scholar, a graduate of Cambridge, England, was cultivated by travel and constant study after he left the University, and yet it was eight years from the time he commenced this poem before he finished it and allowed it, under the most searching revision, to be put in print. But now let us turn to only one of the many psalms unequaled in beauty. Take, for instance, the twenty-third, a psalm of David. It was evidently written at a sitting. It is the production of a man brought up among the flocks and

Gray's Elegy.

[1] C. C. Bombaugh, A.M., M.D.

conversant with the humblest society. He owed little to human training, and had no classical models upon which he might form his style, or from which he might receive his inspiration. "This ode," says Isaac Taylor, "is not to be matched in the circuit of all literature. In its way down through three thousand years or more this psalm has penetrated to the depths of millions of hearts; it has gladdened homes of destitution and discomfort; it has whispered hope and joy amid tears to the utterly solitary and forsaken, whose only refuge was in heaven. Beyond all range of probable calculation have these dozen lines imparted a power of endurance under suffer- Twenty-third psalm. ing, and strength in feebleness, and have kept alive the flickering flame of religious feeling in hearts that were nigh to despair. The divine element herein embodied has given proof, millions of times repeated, of its reality and of its efficacy as a *formula* of tranquil trust in God, and of a grateful sense of his goodness, which all who do trust in him may use for themselves, and use it until it has become assimilated to their own habitual feelings. Thus it is that throughout all time past, and all time to come, this psalm has possessed, and will possess, a life-given virtue toward those who receive it, and whose own path in life is such as life's path most often is."

The renowned philologian Henry Stephanus, who wrote an exposition of the Psalms in 1562, remarks "that in the whole compass of poetry there is nothing more poetical, more musical, more thrilling, and in some pas- Henry Stephanus. sages more full of lofty inspiration than the psalms of David." The great German historian, John von Mueller,

216   THE WORD OF GOD OPENED.

writes in a letter to his brother: "My most delightful hour every day is furnished by David. There is nothing in Greece, nothing in Rome, nothing in all the West like David, who selected the God of Israel to sing him in higher strains than ever praised the gods of the Gentiles. His songs come from the spirit, they sound to the depths of the heart, and never in all my life have I so seen God before my eyes." Alexander von Humboldt, who was a stranger to the Christian faith in the invisible world and to the inward experiences of the Gospel, in his great work entitled "Cosmos," refers to the remarkably truthful representations of nature in Hebrew poetry. He notices especially the one hundred and fourth psalm as presenting "in itself a picture of the whole world." He speaks of the book of Job as being "as graphic in its representations of particular phenomena as it is artistic in the plan of the whole didactic composition," and says of the book of Ruth that it is "a most artless and inexpressibly charming picture of nature." Goëthe says of this same book that it is "the loveliest thing in the shape of an epic or an idyl which has come down to us;" and of the whole volume of inspiration he truthfully testifies, "the Bible becomes more beautiful the more we study it." [2]

John Von Mueller.

Humboldt.

Goethe.

This naturally suggests the analogous thought of the personal influence which the Bible has exercised over the strongest and most original minds. How affecting the tribute paid to it by the unbelieving

Its strong hold upon the most powerful mind.

---

[2] Hagenbach's German Rationalism, page 73. History of the Apostolic Church, page 166.

Rousseau: "This divine book," he says, "the only one which is indispensable to the Christian, need only be read with reflection to inspire love for its Author, and the most ardent desire to obey its precepts. Never did virtue speak so sweet a language, never was the most profound wisdom expressed with so much energy and simplicity. No one can arise from its perusal without feeling himself better than he was before."

Coleridge, in the remarkable letters which he wrote upon the Inspiration of the Bible, which have been the suggestion and seed-thought of most of the tracts issued by the Broad Church party, but which infinitely transcend them in solidity, dignity, richness of thought and expression, and, above all, in humble and loving reverence for the volume of revelation, says, "In the Bible there is more that *finds* me than I have experienced in all other books put together; the words of the Bible find me *at greater depths of my being;* and whatever finds me brings with it an irresistible evidence of its having proceeded from the Holy Spirit." At the close of one of his letters he adds, "The fairest flower that ever clomb up a cottage window is not so fair a sight to my eyes as the Bible gleaming through the lower panes. Let it but be *read*, as by such men it used to be read, when they came to it as to a ground covered with manna—even the bread which the Lord had given his people to eat—where he that gathered much had nothing over, and he that gathered little had no lack. They gathered every man according to his eating. They came to it as to a treasure-house of Scriptures, each

Coleridge's letters.

visitant taking what was precious, and leaving as precious for others."

How affecting the language of Thomas Carlyle, not a too ardent friend of its inspiration, when he says, "David's life and history, as written for us in those psalms of his, I consider to be the truest emblem ever given of a man's moral progress and warfare here below. All earnest souls will ever discern in it the faithful struggles of an earnest human soul toward what is good and best. Struggle often baffled, down as into an entire wreck, yet a struggle never ended; ever with tears, repentance, true, unconquerable purpose, begun anew." Of the book of Job he says, "Noble book; all men's book. It is our first oldest statement of the never-ending problem—man's destiny, and God's ways with him here in the earth. And all in such free, flowing outlines; grand in its sincerity, in its simplicity, in its epic-melody, and repose of reconcilement. So *true* every way, true eye-sight and vision of all things, material things no less than spiritual; the horse—hast thou clothed his neck with *thunder?* he *laughs* at the shaking of the spear. Such living likenesses were never since drawn. Sublime sorrow, sublime reconciliation; oldest choral melody as of the heart of mankind! so soft and great; as the summer midnight, as the world with its seas and stars."

Carlyle's language.

"To all who take up the oracles of God with integrity and honesty," says Bishop Butler, "the Bible will ever possess the peculiarity of meeting every want, and appeasing every difficulty. In its pages every longing of our nature, the most superficial and the

Bishop Butler.

most profound, will find satisfaction. Here provision has been made alike for the tender susceptibility of the child and the mature intellect of manhood; and whatever shadow our imperfect knowledge may allow for the present to rest upon certain of its statements, the mourner will still find solace in the songs of Zion, and philosophy still drink wisdom from the parables of Galilee. It is true that all difficulties may not have been removed which the enemies of Christianity have started; nevertheless, the marvelous success with which most of them have already been met must convince any fair mind that such as still remain are not insurmountable, and that here, if anywhere, it befits our weakness 'to be thankful and to wait.'"

"Read the Bible," says Wilberforce, the statesman, in his dying hour to a friend; "let no religious book take its place. Through all my perplexities and distresses I never read any other book, and I never knew the want of any other. It has been my hourly study; and all my knowledge of the doctrines, and all my acquaintance with the experience and realities of religion, have been derived from the Bible only." *Wilberforce.*

"If any thing I have ever said or written," said Daniel Webster, when commended on a memorable occasion for his eloquence, " deserves the feeblest encomiums of my fellow-countrymen, I have no hesitation in declaring that for their partiality I am indebted, *solely* indebted, to the daily and attentive perusal of the Holy Scriptures, the source of all true poetry and eloquence, as well as of all good and all comfort." *Daniel Webster.*

"Thy creatures," said Sir Francis Bacon, "have been my books, but thy Scriptures much more. I have sought thee in courts, fields, and gardens, but I have found thee in thy temples."

Bacon.

"Let others," said John Milton, "dread and shun the Scriptures for their darkness; I shall wish I may deserve to be reckoned among those who admire and dwell upon them for their clearness."

Milton.

"We account," writes Sir Isaac Newton, "the Scriptures of God to be the most sublime philosophy."

Newton.

Thomas, Lord Erskine writes, "My firm belief in the holy Gospel is by no means owing to the prejudices of education, but it arises from the most continued reflections of my riper years and understanding. It forms at this moment the great consolation of a life which, as a shadow, must pass away."

Lord Erskine.

Says M. Guizot, the truly great and venerable French statesman, in his "Meditations upon the Essence of Christianity," "I have read the sacred volumes over and over again; I have perused them in very different dispositions of mind; at one time studying them as great historical documents, at another admiring them as sublime works of poetry. I have experienced an extraordinary impression quite different from either curiosity or admiration. I have felt myself the listener of a language other than that of the chronicler or the poet, and under the influence of a breath issuing from other sources than human."

Guizot.

The quick-witted but not over-scrupulous Talleyrand, expressed his appreciation of the irre-

Talleyrand.

sistible hold which the Christian Gospel has upon the human mind, when consulted by one of the five directors constituting the French government in 1797, in reference to suitable forms of worship for the new religious system which they had inaugurated, and called Theophilanthropism, (divine humanity,) "I have but a single observation," said Talleyrand, "to make: Jesus Christ, to found his religion, suffered himself to be crucified, and he rose again. You should try to do as much." Only four years afterward remarks Guizot, "Theophilanthropism and its apostle, the dream and the dreamer, had disappeared from the stage, where they had been powerless in influence, barren in consequence."[3]

Time would fail us to recite the voluntary and heartfelt testimonies to the sustaining and inspiring power of the Bible which have come from the noblest minds of all ages in all Christian lands.

The Bible has indeed in it, combined in the highest degree, what Matthew Arnold quotes from Swift as the two noblest of things, *sweetness* and *light*.

What volume of human origin could endure the ordeal of constant reading and study, and exhaust a life-time in its investigation, supplying until the last increasing stimulation and comfort? Thousands of commentators and critical scholars have devoted their intellectual lives to the study of the Holy Scriptures, and have ceased, like the venerable Bede, at once to work and live; consecrating their last breath to the translation or illustration of the Bible

[3] Meditations on the Actual State of Christianity.

Prof. Calvin Stowe, in his very interesting volume entitled "The Origin and History of the Books of the Bible," refers to this line of thought. "Let us bring," he says, "this matter to the test of fact and common sense. These men say the Bible is no more inspired than the writings of Homer and Shakspeare, and other great men whom God has fitted to be the instructors of mankind. Well, then, let us try and see. Let us for a while use Homer and Shakspeare instead of the Bible, say night and morning, in our family prayers. When we meet in the house of God for his worship; in the hour of sickness and calamity and distress; at funerals, when all our earthly hopes are blighted, and we lay our dearest friends in the grave; let us then, instead of reading the Bible, take a few passages from Homer and Shakspeare. How long do you think this would last before we should be glad to get back to our Bible again?"

<small>Other books tried in the place of the Bible.</small>

A book that has so imbedded itself in all literature and science; that has for nearly two thousand years sustained its claim to a divine origin; that has exercised so marvelous an influence over human society, and impressed itself so powerfully upon the strongest thinkers of every age, has little to fear from the hasty generalizations of modern science, or from the passionate attacks of a superficial criticism, which exposes its object and animus in the irreverent and reckless style in which it has clothed itself. To these self-confident modern Gnostics, who demand the reason why these things should not be believed, we may answer as Henry Moore did Southey when he inquired of him,

<small>A book thus imbedded in the world's literature cannot die.</small>

"Why am not I qualified to write a biography of John Wesley?" "Sir, thou hast nothing to draw with, and the well is deep."

We close this volume with the well-known lines of Walter Scott, said to have been written in his Bible:

> Within this awful volume lies
> The mystery of mysteries;
> O! happiest they of human race,
> To whom our God has given grace
> To hear, to read, to fear, to pray,
> To lift the latch and force the way;
> But better had they ne'er been born
> Who read to doubt, or read to scorn.

THE END.

www.ingramcontent.com/pod-product-compliance
Lightning Source LLC
Chambersburg PA
CBHW031819230426
43669CB00009B/1188